Embracing a Life of Abundance

Embracing a
Life of Abundance

Find Yourself, Accept Yourself, Give Yourself Away

Tim Gott, EdD

tandem light press

Tandem Light Press
950 Herrington Rd.
Suite C128
Lawrenceville, GA 30044

Copyright © 2023 by Tim Gott

All rights reserved. No part of this book may be reproduced, scanned, or transmitted in any printed, electronic, or mechanical, including photocopying, recording, or any information storage and retrieval system, without permission in writing from the publisher. Please do not participate in or encourage piracy of copyrighted materials in violation of the author's rights.

The content of this book is for informational purposes only and is not intended to diagnose, treat, cure, or prevent any condition or disease. You understand that this book is not intended as a substitute for consultation with a licensed practitioner. Please consult with your physician or healthcare specialist regarding the suggestions and recommendations made in this book.

Tandem Light Press paperback edition Summer 2023

ISBN: 979-8-9856404-8-9

PRINTED IN THE UNITED STATES OF AMERICA

To the love of my life, Ellen.
You have taught me what true love is.

"The best way to find yourself is to lose yourself in the service of others."

–Mahatma Gandhi

CONTENTS

Foreword	xi
Preface	xiii
Acknowledgments	xv
Introduction	xvii
Part I: Finding and Accepting Ourselves	1
Looking at the Whole	3
Looking at the Four Strands Separately	9
Physical	10
Mental	23
Emotional	41
Spiritual	47
Part II: Giving Ourselves Away	63
Relationships	65
Work	83
Daily Life	96
Conclusion	103
Recommended Reading	105
Bibliography	107
About the Author	111

FOREWORD

It is with great pleasure that I introduce *Embracing a Life of Abundance: Find Yourself, Accept Yourself, Give Yourself Away* by my esteemed colleague, Dr. Tim Gott. In this book, Dr. Gott presents a holistic approach to finding balance and alignment in our lives by exploring the four fundamental strands of being human: physical, mental, emotional, and spiritual. With over thirty-eight years of experience as an educator, coach, and leader, Dr. Gott's insights and expertise are invaluable in guiding readers on their journey towards self-discovery and fulfillment.

In the first part of the book, Dr. Gott emphasizes the importance of assessing our health and balance in each of these fundamental strands of being human. He guides readers through the process of exploring each strand individually while simultaneously highlighting their interconnectedness. By focusing on the wholeness of our being, Dr. Gott helps us find and accept ourselves.

In the second part of the book, Dr. Gott extends his approach to the broader context of relationships, work, and daily life. He demonstrates how, by establishing our sense of balance and alignment, we can cultivate that into our relationships, our work, and our daily lives. Dr. Gott challenges us to examine what healthy connections look like with ourselves, with others, and with that which is beyond us. He encourages us to find meaning and purpose by fulfilling our personal mission and service, and he inspires us to embrace a mindset of abundance.

As an ICF credentialed coach and now faculty of the Academy of Creative Coaching, Dr. Gott's work has impacted the lives of countless individuals. His commitment to encouraging and supporting others in reaching their goals and living out their purpose is evident in every page of this book. I have no doubt that readers will find his insights and expertise invaluable as they embark on their own journey towards self-discovery and fulfillment.

Dr. Gott's expertise, coupled with his great integrity and commitment to excellence, makes this book a must-read for anyone seeking to find balance and alignment in their lives. I highly recommend it.

– Dr. Pamela Larde, PhD, CPC

Founder and President of the Academy of Creative Coaching
Director of Education for the McLean/Harvard Medical School Institute of Coaching

ACKNOWLEDGMENTS

This book has been in the making for over thirty years. It has been deeply influenced by the multitude of people who have been in my life over this time. First and foremost, I would like to thank my wife, Ellen, who has kept the fire burning in me with her support, insight, and patience. When I would lose interest or feel unworthy to be a writer, her words of encouragement and gentle nudges to move forward kept the spark alive within me.

I am truly grateful for my children and their spouses, Andrew and Lauren, Emily and Jason, and Ryan and Megan, who have also served to inspire me in my writing. Their own journeys have taught me much about what it means to find your true self. I am grateful for their love and tolerance as I have wrestled with finding and accepting myself.

Much of what is in this book began as conversations with my students and staff over the years. I am indebted to them for putting up with my random wanderings and being my captured audience at times as I tried to formulate many of the ideas found in this book. I carry fond memories and affection for everyone who let me walk with them along their educational path.

I would like to also thank some key individuals who challenged me at various times to write a book: Mrs. Estelle Wheat, my high school English teacher; Carol Christian, fellow HSE and accomplished writer; Chris Wagner, my dissertation chair; Stephanie Haynes, my peer coach; Lee Watts, a friend and marketing guru; and Caroline Smith, my author coach.

And finally, to all of the wonderful folks who have read my newsletters, blog posts, and articles over the years, thanks for helping me believe that I had something worthwhile to share with the world.

INTRODUCTION

All of us travel a unique path while we are on this planet. I have had the opportunity to work as a math teacher, high school counselor, K-12 principal, and as a leadership and life coach. I have shared this run so far with a wonderful partner of over thirty-six years and we have raised three remarkable children. I have also been fortunate to travel to many amazing places around the world. All my experiences have provided a rich foundation for me to see patterns and connections across diverse aspects of life. This has led me to a profound desire to understand myself and others more fully. While my story is different from anyone else's, I have found that we all can learn from one another by sharing our life lessons along the way. It is in this spirit that I offer this book to those who may find common ground with me.

Over my lifetime, a particular phrase has become a guiding principle for me:

Find yourself, Accept yourself, Give yourself away.

For me, this speaks to the need for each of us to come to know who we are at our deepest core. From that connection with our authentic selves, we then must come to accept both the potential and the limitations of being ourselves. Out of this self-awareness, we then are empowered to give ourselves away through meaningful relationships, purposeful work, and abundant living.

Richard Bach wrote in his book *Illusions,* "Our only obligation in life is to be true to ourselves." This idea really bothered me for much of my early life. It sounded so selfish. However, at this stage in my journey, it resonates deeply within me. Fundamentally, the most important journey we can take is inward. Until we seek to know our true selves, we are battered by all the currents of shoulds, have-tos, and others' opinions. We create incongruence in our lives when we are out of alignment with who we really are. This breach of integrity is the root of most of our struggles in life.

To find wholeness, balance, and congruence, we must be willing to do the hard work of exploring our very nature and embracing what we find. It is from this continual process that we can find our true independence from the things that pull us out of alignment. With a deeper understanding of who we are, we can seek interdependent relationships that bring joy and meaning to our lives.

One of the most important aspects of this process to remember is that this is an ongoing journey of discovery and evolution. We are not who we were yesterday. Today is another piece in the mosaic of our growth and becoming. For much of my life, I pursued what I thought everyone else wanted or needed me to be. I only felt valuable or worthy when I was pleasing someone else. When that didn't work, I believed I was a failure. In the last few years, an ironic transition has happened. When I let go of trying to earn my place in the world by pleasing everyone and focusing on perfection, I found the true inspiration to make a difference in the world. By seeing myself honestly and holistically, I have learned to love myself for who I am. Accepting my strengths and my flaws, I have been freed of unrealistic shackles and the burdens of living up to everyone else's standards and expectations. Instead, I can give myself to others in authentic ways that are mutually beneficial for everyone.

Daniel Goleman talks about this process as the elements of emotional intelligence (EQ). EQ requires that we first have a strong self-awareness that leads to effective self-management. Once we understand ourselves more, we can extend our comprehension to others through empathy and social awareness. This broader, external focus enables us to interact with others in positive and purposeful connections. This includes our closest personal relationships, our friendships, our teamwork, and our leadership capacity.

Using EQ as a foundation, I have been developing a framework for sustaining congruence in my life. This book is essentially an outline of how to establish and maintain integrity and alignment.

This book consists of two main parts: **Finding & Accepting Ourselves** and **Giving Ourselves Away**. In the first part, we will start by looking holistically at the four fundamental strands of being human: physical, mental, emotional, and spiritual, and we will then explore them individually. These four are equally important and are intricately connected. While it is important to see how the strands work together, it is helpful to also look at them separately for the purpose of assessing our health and balance in each one.

After we explore the individual strands, we will bring the focus back on the wholeness and interconnection of each of them.

In part two, we will explore what it means to give ourselves away. Having established our individual sense of balance and alignment, we will extend that into our relationships, our work, and our daily lives. In terms of relationships, we will examine what healthy connections look like with ourselves, with others, and with that which is beyond us. In terms of work, we will dive into finding meaning and purpose by fulfilling our personal mission and service. Finally, we will look at seeing our daily lives holistically and how to embrace a mindset of abundance.

A professor once shared with me that you can't teach truth directly. I have found that stories and metaphors have helped me understand fundamental principles at deeper levels. It is my hope that my reflections, experiences, and insights will serve as catalysts and jumping-off points for your own journey. While I truly believe what I have shared here, I am fully aware that it is still an incomplete and biased worldview based on my life journey. As such, use these words as they best fit your growth. If just one thing in here helps you move in a positive direction, I will have accomplished the purpose of this book.

– Tim

Part I:

Finding and Accepting Ourselves

Moving from Dependency to Independency

Looking at the Whole

In Martha Beck's book, *The Way of Integrity*, she speaks of the divided self. As a math teacher, when I hear "divided," the word congruence comes to mind. For me, being congruent means that our inner world aligns fully with our outer expression of ourselves. So many of our life struggles come from the incongruency of who we really are and what we project to the world. We each grapple with the tension between authenticity and cultural expectations. When these clash, we learn to wear masks. From an early age, we often choose to sacrifice who we are so that we can be what we think everyone else wants us to be. Gone unchecked over the years of our lives, we may find ourselves looking in the mirror and wondering who is looking back. This duplicity can create many of our physical, mental, emotional, and spiritual health issues. Many authors, including Beck, share their journeys and suggest pathways to reveal and heal our divided selves.

One of the things that keeps emerging in my life is that our bodies and the universe actually are talking to us. In multiple ways, they are showing us paths to restoration and reconciliation—if we can find ways to truly listen despite our fear, defensiveness, and stubbornness. It begins with opening up to the possibility that we don't know it all and that we may need to reevaluate much of what we believe to be true. In this openness, we create space for genuine reflection and recognition of who we really are. When we can see what is authentic versus what is a mask, we allow ourselves to move toward wholeness and integrity.

To be able to live an abundant life, we need to start by examining the interconnectedness of the physical, mental, emotional, and spiritual elements of who we are. For me, physical means the body, the five senses, and the various biological and neurological systems at work internally; mental is the way we think and process information; emotional is the range and depth of our feelings; and spiritual refers to our acquired beliefs and values. To find balance and harmony within ourselves, we need to assess how functional we are in each of these strands on a regular basis.

ETFBC

Neuroscientists have significantly advanced the field of understanding these four strands and how they dynamically interact. One model of how our systems work with the world follows this pathway: Experience – Thought – Feeling – Behavior – Consequences (ETFBC)

I like to think of the relationship of these elements as a four-legged stool. When it is sitting solidly on all four legs, the stool is fully functional and can serve its purpose. If any of the legs are shorter or missing, it throws everything off. In my classes and presentations, I often balance a stool on one of its legs in my hand to demonstrate the difficulty and awkwardness of trying to live our lives focusing only on one strand.

The four elements are working in connection with one another through the ETFBC process. Physically, we experience an event or a situation. We take in information through our senses. Mentally, we interact with this information through a wide variety of thinking processes. We begin to filter the data through our neural pathways. Simultaneously, we take the incoming knowledge and go through a comparative process to our beliefs and values. Our brains receive the data, process it, and evaluate it, almost instantaneously. The next product of this process is an emotional response. Our feelings can range from very mild to dangerously explosive. Out of this emotional state, we react, sometimes positively, sometimes not. Our behavior then produces consequences that we must live with.

When we look at this sequence from an outside perspective, we see that the critical link in the process is our thoughts. We don't often have control over the experiences that we encounter. However, how we think about these is on us. Brené Brown refers to this as the space between stimulus and response. We may not be aware of how we are mentally addressing a situation, but we can learn to. Through personal study or professional support, we can come to recognize our thoughts and respond in beneficial ways. In doing so, we influence the outcomes of our feelings, behaviors, and consequences.

Here is an example of the process. Hiking on a trail, you encounter a snake. This is the experience step. Then, the thought process kicks in. Each of us may have a different experience. For some, the initial thought is a threat. Your belief system engages. Maybe you believe that snakes are dangerous and should be avoided at all costs. This leads to an emotional response. Possibly, fear arises within you. Your behavior could be that you scream and run or freeze and wet yourself. Depending on the environment, the consequences could be embarrassing or physically harmful if you fall or twist an ankle as you flee.

If the thought process was different, the results could be affected. For instance, the initial response could be a positive one. You might like snakes. You stop and observe it and enjoy the moment. The consequence might be insignificant or, potentially, you might get bit because of lack of caution. In any event, the initial thinking stage majorly influences the outcome.

So, what's the point? We experience multiple situations daily. We ride a roller coaster of thoughts and feelings. If we seek to understand the underlying processes that are going on within us, we can find ways to handle the days in more productive and beneficial ways. Using the ETFBC sequence allows us to assess prior events in our lives so that we can make positive changes in the way we live. Knowing that our thoughts are the leverage point in the process gives us control of our lives. We may not be able to change the external conditions around us, but we can change the way we think about them. When we own this idea, we empower ourselves to deal with whatever comes more effectively. Let's look at some other concepts that underlie this process.

Need Theory

Abraham Maslow was an American psychologist (1908–1970) who introduced humanistic psychology. His work sought to see human development from a positive viewpoint as opposed to the deficit focus of prior psychological theories such as the work of Freud. One of the major concepts that Maslow introduced was a hierarchy of needs. He never actually used a triangular model for the theory, but it emerged from others sharing his work. He saw these needs as more fluid and overlapping. However, his work helps us articulate and visualize the criticalness of meeting our basic needs. The basic premise is that for us to be fully actualized human beings, we must have our physical, psychological, relational, and esteem needs met. Each of these needs depends and builds on the earlier ones.

If we integrate the four strands of being human into his hierarchy, we can see how physical, mental, emotional, and spiritual needs connect. Fundamentally, the idea is that we cannot reach our full potential or live fully with our integrity if we are unable to meet these needs. It certainly makes sense that if we are physically ill or threatened that everything else seems minimized. If we are psychologically at risk, it has the same impact of keeping us from living a more holistic life. However, when we are physiologically and psychologically safe and sound, we can focus on building relationships, creating meaning and purpose, and contributing positively to the world.

So, when we seek to determine whether we are living congruently and in balance across the four strands, one of the key areas to assess is how well are our needs being met. More importantly, are we aware of what it takes to meet those needs? In the following sections, we will focus on defining those needs and finding ways to meet them in congruence with our true selves.

Looking at the Four Strands Separately

In my journey to find myself, I have had moments of clarity of what balance looks like across the four strands but, more often than not, something is always lagging in at least one area. I move in and out of being physically fit. I have struggled with my weight over the years. I go in cycles of building good habits around exercise despite knowing better since I was an athletic coach in my earlier days. Yet, I drop off regularly every year. I have struggled with my mental health throughout my life and have only come to a deeper understanding of what I need to work on since my mid-fifties. My emotional balance has teetered back and forth as I have wrestled with anger issues and low-level anxiety most of my life. My spiritual well-being has been majorly impacted by my experiences and relationships. Suffice it to say, I don't have all the answers. I continue to be a work in process. However, through my mistakes and successes, I have discovered some things that have made a significant difference in my life. In the following sections, I'll share some of those major insights.

Let's start by looking at some fundamentals of each strand, some of the research in these areas that inform us on how to better live within these strands, and some of the barriers and pitfalls that keep us from living congruently in each area. While the order of the elements is somewhat arbitrary, I have chosen this sequence: physical, mental, emotional, and spiritual because it aligns with the flow of Maslow's hierarchy in my mind. Once again, these are all integrated with each other when we are functioning fully; however, it is helpful to assess each individually as a starting point.

PHYSICAL

My physical journey over my lifetime can best be described as a roller coaster ride. As a high school and college student, I was driven to stay in shape. I started college weighing around 160 and felt invincible. I ate everything in sight and rarely worried about my health. Going to school at Western Kentucky University, it was not difficult to stay active. We aren't called the Hilltoppers for nothing. Walking and running up and down the campus, I kept a decent balance physically. However, when I started my teaching career and began my young adult life, working out slipped way down my daily agenda. I distinctly remember one of the girls I coached in track calling me the "Pillsbury Doughboy." By my early thirties, I was in the mid-180s. By age forty, I was over 200 pounds. I want to emphasize here that weight is not an issue in itself. However, for me, it has been a tangible indicator of my health struggles.

During this time, I convinced myself that I carried the weight fairly well on my 5'8" stocky frame. However, my terrible eating habits and sporadic exercise routines eventually caught up with me. The first incident that shook me up happened in my early forties. One Monday morning at my office, I began to feel a strange sensation spread across my chest and up into my neck. It wasn't painful actually, just very uncomfortable. I began to feel flush. After talking with my wife and a couple of people in the office, I decided to go to the hospital. Over the next several hours, I went through a series of tests, passed out at one point, and ended up staying the night in the ICU. Fortunately, my heart turned out fine, but my blood work revealed several issues including extremely high triglycerides (upper 700s). It may have had something to do with the three cheeseburgers and two bowls of ice cream I had eaten the night before. One of the worst things that came out of the event was that I had to miss my daughter's Washington DC trip later in the week, something I regret to this day.

I would love to be able to say that my life turned around fully from this, but it didn't. I did start exercising more and trying to eat better, but I fell back into the same habits that had led me to that situation. Over the next fifteen years, I fluctuated from 205 to 228 like a yo-yo. I was on a "See-Food" diet; if I saw it, I ate it. I would go through short cycles of trying to move back into a healthy balance, but I could not sustain it. If we don't listen to the messages our bodies are sending us, they will speak even louder. For me, the next substantial health crisis happened in my mid-50s.

Due to a wide range of life circumstances that included me not handling stress well and choosing to ignore red flags along the way, my intestines nearly ruptured due to diverticulitis. After spending two days in the hospital and narrowly avoiding major surgery, I finally got the message that my life patterns had to change. Over the following six months, I lost over thirty pounds, started walking consistently every day, and began to minimize my sugar intake (I found out I was prediabetic).

Since then, I have felt better than I have for most of my adult life. It is important to mention that my physical journey cannot be disconnected from everything that was going on with me mentally, emotionally, and spiritually. Each of these strands was deeply involved. However, for this section, I wanted to focus specifically on my physical health as the context for the material that follows. I would like to share several of the resources, skills, and habits that I have found that improved my life in meaningful ways. While I hope these suggestions are

Physical Needs

I suspect you are a lot like me—we take our physical needs for granted. What's interesting is: we can live approximately thirty days without food, we might live about three days without water, and about three minutes without air. It is amazing how getting sick can bring the importance of this domain into focus. Nothing else seems to be important when you are lying on the bathroom floor after a stomach virus has invaded your body. But we quickly minimize our physical balance when we are healthy again. So, it is necessary to take inventory regularly of how we are functioning in the areas of our physical needs which include hydration, nutrition, warmth & shelter, sleep, and exercise.

Maslow found that our physical needs are the foundation from which we build everything else. With years of research and case studies, we know, for the most part, what we need to do to stay physically balanced. However, for a variety of reasons, many of us struggle to maintain our physical health on a regular basis. To assess how aligned we are to where we need to be in this domain, let's start with examining what researchers recommend across our physical needs. I want to acknowledge that these next pages may be things that you already know and are possibly doing. It may also feel a little too clinical. However, since the physical strand is fundamental for the other strands to function well, it is an important first step.

Water

One of the best things I did for myself was to start drinking water more and minimizing other beverages. We truly underestimate the impact water has on our health. Water is the most important compound on the planet. It makes up over

70% of the earth. It makes up 60% of the human body and 90% of the brain. Experts say that drinking water is the healthiest thing we can do for ourselves. Here are five benefits of water as mentioned in an article from UC Health online[1]:

1. **Water boosts energy**. Water delivers important nutrients to all of our cells, especially muscle cells, postponing muscle fatigue.

2. **Water helps weight loss**. Water helps you feel full longer, without adding any additional calories. Drinking water or eating foods with a high-water content can be a big help in managing your weight.

3. **Water aids in digestion**. Water aids in constipation and other abdominal issues, especially those suffering from IBS. Water helps to move the digestive process along and through the system.

4. **Water detoxifies**. Moves toxins through your system faster and optimizes kidney function. Inadequate hydration means inadequate kidney function.

5. **Water hydrates skin**. Forget expensive creams and cure-alls, water is the best defense against aging and wrinkles in the skin.

Essentially, when we take in the appropriate amount of water each day, we are maintaining the most effective component of a healthy system in the body. Depending on our height and weight, taking in around eight cups of water a day is a good average. Water intake can be supplemented by eating fruits and

---

[1] UCHealth Writers, "Five Reasons Water Is So Important to Your Health," UCHealth Today, November 2, 2021, https://www.uchealth.org/today/five-reasons-water-is-so-important-to-your-health/.

vegetables which have high water content. Drinking other beverages in moderation is acceptable, depending on medical conditions. Avoiding drinks high in sugar and minimizing alcohol consumption helps maintain a healthier balance.

Food

I love food. I have had a chance to eat some of the best meals in the world. Unfortunately, moderation is not a word that I understand very well. When I eat appropriate servings, I definitely feel better. When I don't, my system talks to me loudly. One of my biggest issues is that eating is a way of coping with stress and anxiety. Becoming aware of how my eating was impacting my mental health gave me a strong foundation to develop better eating habits.

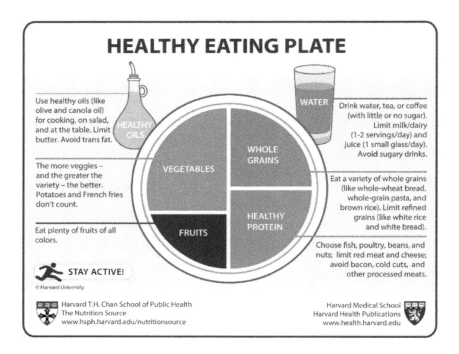

If we want to have a better relationship with food, we don't have to look very far. Strangely, eating the right foods is probably the most communicated information regarding physical health. The push begins in elementary school and continues to appear throughout our lives. With education, support, and a genuine desire to do better, the pathway is clear. The basic premise can be represented by the previous chart from the Harvard Medical School.

For many, eating a healthy balance of foods is complicated by access and financial limitations. However, we can work on increasing the beneficial items from the prescribed "plate" and minimizing the less helpful foods.

Warmth and Shelter

Have you ever been so cold that you shiver? If so, you have experienced the beginning of hypothermia. In my ignorance as a young man, I put myself in harm's way a few times by camping out in the cold. One particular fishing trip in early spring, I came close to a point of no return. Having slept in a minimal tent and sleeping bag during a below freezing night, my fishing partner and I got out on the misty lake early the next morning. As the cold wetness settled into my bones, I began to shake violently, and my hands were dysfunctional. Realizing that things were going south quickly, we made our way to a cabin. Getting into a warm place, eating some hot food, and getting out of wet clothes probably saved me. However, it still took hours before I could truly function again. This experience taught me how we rarely even think about our physical environment.

Being warm and safe is something we may take for granted every day. However, our daily interactions are impacted greatly by how we regulate our temperature and the safety of where we live. For a typical adult, normal body temperature ranges from 97 F to 99 F. Babies and children have a little higher range: 97.9 F to 100.4 F. The human capacity to maintain body temperature is a fantastic system at work. It is resilient and powerful. However, it is not infallible. Being too cold (hypothermia) or too hot (hyperthermia) can be life-threatening quickly. To provide an optimal environment for healthy living, indoor temperatures should range between 64–75 degrees F (18–24° C).[2]

Where we lay our head down at night varies widely. For many of us, this is another thing that we rarely consider once we have a set place we call home. To have a safe environment in which to live is a privilege that the majority of people on the planet do not experience. During my years working in schools, I observed many families that lacked the essentials, just doors down from well-equipped homes. If we live where there is protection from the elements, clean drinking water, heating and air-conditioning, and a non-violent community, we need to stop and remember to be grateful for these opportunities and be mindful of those around us that are in need. We have it within our capacity to ensure that everyone has a safe place to live.

Exercise

We all know that we need to exercise, but we each can find a thousand excuses that keep us from getting the amount of physical fitness we need. Personally, I have struggled with setting aside time to work out. In my head, I use to believe that my routines needed to be intense and exhausting. The real aha for me was realizing that a little exercise every day goes a long way. Just walking for 15–30 minutes a day can transform our bodies. I have found this to be true by starting most days with

---

[2] Fermin Koop, "Not Too Hot, Not Too Cold. What's the Ideal Room Temperature?," ZME Science, March 9, 2023, https://www.zmescience.com/other/feature-post/not-too-hot-not-too-cold-whats-the-ideal-room-temperature/.

a short walk around my neighborhood. Carving out that little window of time first thing in the morning has allowed me to not only get needed exercise but it is a meaningful time to think and reflect on the coming day.

Each of us can find small windows of time to integrate a few healthy routines daily. It may be helpful to know that the American Heart Association recommends these guidelines for adults and children:

Recommendations for Adults[3]

- Get at least 150 minutes per week of moderate-intensity aerobic activity or 75 minutes per week of vigorous aerobic activity, or a combination of both preferably spread throughout the week.
- Add moderate- to high-intensity muscle-strengthening activity (such as resistance or weights) at least 2 days per week.
- Spend less time sitting. Even light-intensity activity can offset some of the risks of being sedentary.
- Gain even more benefits by being active for at least 300 minutes (five hours) per week.
- Increase the amount and intensity gradually over time.

Recommendations for Kids

- Children 3–5 years old should be physically active and have plenty of opportunities to move throughout the day.

---

[3] "American Heart Association Recommendations for Physical Activity in Adults and Kids," www.heart.org, July 28, 2022, https://www.heart.org/en/healthy-living/

- Kids 6–17 years old should get at least 60 minutes per day of moderate- to vigorous-intensity physical activity, mostly aerobic.
- Include vigorous-intensity activity on at least three days per week.
- Include muscle- and bone-strengthening (weight-bearing) activities at least three days per week.
- Increase the amount and intensity gradually over time.

Sleep

Working with students over the years, I have seen the daily impact of people not getting enough sleep. Somehow in our culture, we have associated sleep with laziness. We wear our lack of sleep as a badge of honor. We often brag about how little sleep we can "function" on. However, in recent years, research has shown how the lack of sleep may be one of the most detrimental things we experience. To frame it more positively, the medical community emphasizes that one of the first steps we need to take for a balanced and healthy lifestyle is to establish a regular and consistent sleep pattern. With some variation due to age, most of us need around 7–9 hours of sleep a day. While we are sleeping, we are allowing our bodies to recharge, heal, and process our food for nutrition and sustainability. By minimizing sleep, we short-circuit our brains, throw off our metabolism, and weaken our immune system. According to an article from Sleep Foundation[4], sleep provides these 8 health benefits:

- Improved Mood
- Healthy Heart
- Regulated Blood Sugar
- Improved Mental Function

---

[4] "Eight Health Benefits of Sleep," Sleep Foundation, April 15, 2022, https://www.sleepfoundation.org/how-sleep-works/benefits-of-sleep.

- Restored Immune System
- Stress Relief
- Athletic Performance
- Maintaining Healthy Weight

All of us have experienced those nights when we wake up at 2 am and our thoughts have hijacked our bodies. Lying in bed and watching the clock every few minutes is pretty miserable. I have found that when I am stressed and anxious, I am very likely to have a 1–1 ½ hour window where I cannot fall back to sleep.

The Mayo Clinic recommends these practices for better sleep[5]:

1. Stick to a sleep schedule

Set aside no more than eight hours for sleep. The recommended amount of sleep for a healthy adult is at least seven hours. Most people don't need more than eight hours in bed to be well rested.

Go to bed and get up at the same time every day, including weekends. Being consistent reinforces your body's sleep-wake cycle.

If you don't fall asleep within about 20 minutes of going to bed, leave your bedroom and do something relaxing. Read or listen to soothing music. Go back to bed when you're tired. Repeat as needed but continue to maintain your sleep schedule and wake-up time.

---

[5] "6 Steps to Better Sleep," Mayo Clinic (Mayo Foundation for Medical Education and Research, May 7, 2022), https://www.mayoclinic.org/

2. Pay attention to what you eat and drink

Don't go to bed hungry or stuffed. In particular, avoid heavy or large meals within a couple of hours of bedtime. Discomfort might keep you up.

Nicotine, caffeine, and alcohol deserve caution, too. The stimulating effects of nicotine and caffeine take hours to wear off and can interfere with sleep. And even though alcohol might make you feel sleepy at first, it can disrupt sleep later in the night.

3. Create a restful environment

Keep your room cool, dark, and quiet. Exposure to light in the evenings might make it more challenging to fall asleep. Avoid prolonged use of light-emitting screens just before bedtime. Consider using room-darkening shades, earplugs, a fan, or other devices to create an environment that suits your needs.

Doing calming activities before bedtime, such as taking a bath or using relaxation techniques, might promote better sleep.

4. Limit daytime naps

Long daytime naps can interfere with nighttime sleep. Limit naps to no more than one hour and avoid napping late in the day.

However, if you work nights, you might need to nap late in the day before work to help make up your sleep debt.

5. Include physical activity in your daily routine

Regular physical activity can promote better sleep. However, avoid being active too close to bedtime.

Spending time outside every day might be helpful, too.

6. Manage worries

Try to resolve your worries or concerns before bedtime. Jot down what's on your mind and then set it aside for tomorrow.

Stress management might help. Start with the basics, such as getting organized, setting priorities, and delegating tasks. Meditation also can ease anxiety.

Wrapping Up

When all these elements are taken into consideration, we have a broader picture of what a healthy body could be. Remember, it may take a substantial amount of time and an intentional effort to create congruence physically. Choose one area to start with and make small changes each day. Over time, we can establish healthier habits that are sustainable and enriching. Here are some things that I have found to be beneficial for me:

- Walk every day. I try to average 3-4 miles a day.
- Choose water most of the time.
- Eat a balanced diet and work on moderation (still struggling with this one).
- Go to bed at the same time every evening.
- Practice mindfulness through breathing exercises and meditation.

Activities

1. Track your water intake for three days. If you find that your daily quantity is lacking, add just one more glass of water a day for a week. In the second week, add another. Continue until you are taking in the proper amount for yourself.
2. Get a full physical
3. Take the Mayo Clinic Fitness Self-Assessment:

https://www.mayoclinic.org/healthy-lifestyle/fitness/in-depth/fitness/art-20046433

4. Take the 4-Part Health Test: https://www.washingtonpost.com/health/the-longevity-files-a-strong-grip-pushups-what-actually-can-help-you-live-to-a-ripe-old-age/2019/09/27/e2cffb5c-da34-11e9-ac63-3016711543fe_story.html

5. Take a sleep assessment: https://assets.nhs.uk/tools/self-assessments/index.mob.html?variant=72

MENTAL

I have been fascinated with how the brain works since my early days in school. This incredible biological system continues to draw my curiosity. As a student, I found great joy in striving to maximize my capacity to remember content and solve problems. I was the nerd who loved tests and couldn't wait to be challenged each year. My early success served as a launch pad for my adult life and my career as an educator. In my work, I found it to be critically important to know what is going on inside our heads so that I could help my students learn at deeper levels. Each year, I discover new information and research that broadens my understanding of the incredible machine called the brain.

However, along with my academic growth and development, I have come to realize the shadow side of my mental health. Like many people, for many years, I never internalized that my thinking was a system at work instead of a bank of absolute truth. Like any system, it can only function long-term if each piece or component within the framework maintains its integrity. My arrogance and pride kept me from seeing that many of my beliefs and thoughts were incomplete, misguided, or just wrong. I felt that if it was my thought, it had to be true. Breaking away from this mindset has been one of the most freeing and restorative things I have ever done.

With a lifetime of experiences and study, I have come to understand more about the brain and how our thinking works or doesn't work. The following sections represent much of what I have gathered over the years.

The Science of Thinking

The mental strand is essentially defined as how we process information. Neuroscience and educational research have continued to reveal how the human brain takes in data and integrates it into daily life processes. It is critically important to emphasize that our mental processes are mechanical and systemic; they are not infallible and absolute. Put another way, just because we think something doesn't make it true. However, understanding the system helps us know how to use our thinking more effectively.

The following chart gives a broad overview of how our brain operates in gathering information and storing it in memory.

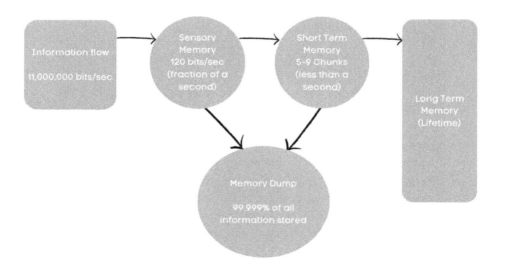

At any given moment, 11,000,000 bits of information bombard our brains per second. That's 11 million! For the most part, we flush all of that out immediately. Depending on our age, we might process 120 bits per sec at any moment, which cluster into five to nine chunks of information. Depending on various circumstances, we might push that into long-term memory or just let those bits go like the rest. For instance, we may be talking to someone. We hear them, see them, possibly smell them, and juggle that sensory cocktail in that instance. Depending on how important or engaging the conversation is, we may lock into what they are saying and remember it forever. More often than not, though, it will just fade quickly out of our memory.

Research shows that these are some of the factors that help us move things into long-term memory:

- Emotional connection
- Need for survival
- Novelty
- Related to other things already in our long-term memory
- Repetition
- Music
- Multisensory interaction

Having some basic knowledge of how information is stored in our brains can broaden our understanding of how our thinking works. When we look at our mental capacities from that foundation, we find that there is also shape and complexity to the system at work. Some of the dynamics include context, depth, and breadth. In terms of context, the work of Howard Gardner on multiple intelligences expands our understanding of how intelligence has many facets. I have been fascinated with Gardner's work as an educator because it allows each of us to see that we can be "smart" in many diverse ways. As a mathematician and a counselor, I found that the logical-mathematical intelligence as well as the interpersonal one spoke to how I processed the world. I also could see the others working in my thinking as well at times. It is very affirming that we all have each of these intelligences. While we may favor certain ones more, the brain is more engaged when we highlight each of these as we learn.

The Nine Multiple Intelligences[6]

- Verbal-linguistic intelligence (well-developed verbal skills and sensitivity to the sounds, meanings, and rhythms of words)
- Logical-mathematical intelligence (ability to think conceptually and abstractly, and capacity to discern logical and numerical patterns)
- Spatial-visual intelligence (capacity to think in images and pictures, to visualize accurately and abstractly)
- Bodily-kinesthetic intelligence (ability to control one's body movements and to handle objects skillfully)
- Musical intelligence (ability to produce and appreciate rhythm, pitch, and timber)
- Interpersonal intelligence (capacity to detect and respond appropriately to the moods, motivations, and desires of others)
- Intrapersonal (capacity to be self-aware and in tune with inner feelings, values, beliefs, and thinking processes)
- Naturalist intelligence (ability to recognize and categorize plants, animals, and other objects in nature)
- Existential intelligence (sensitivity and capacity to tackle deep questions about human existence such as, "What

---

[6] "Concept to Classroom: Tapping into Multiple Intelligences," Concept to classroom: Tapping into multiple intelligences - explanation, 2004, https://www.thirteen.org/edonline/concept2class/mi/index.html.

is the meaning of life? Why do we die? How did we get here?") [7]

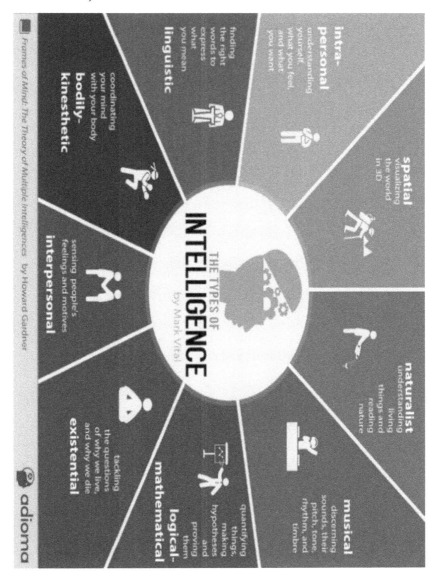

---

[7] "The Teaching and Learning Center," UTHSC, accessed April 6, 2023, https://uthsc.edu/tlc/.

In terms of depth, Benjamin Bloom is famous for developing a taxonomy that emphasizes different levels of higher-order thinking.

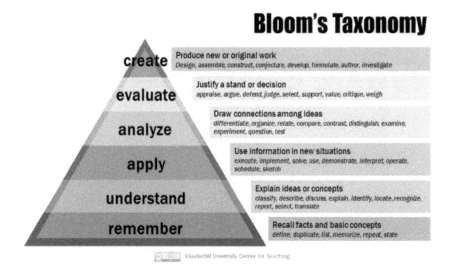

If we want to strengthen our thinking skills, focusing on the depth of our thoughts as we seek to understand and implement knowledge can have a major impact. The more we utilize application, analysis, evaluation, and creation, the stronger the neuropathways connected to specific content become. It is important to also remember that to use higher-order thinking skills most effectively, we must have a strong foundation in basic knowledge and comprehension of the content first.

For example, let's take earning money in a savings account. At first, we may learn about earning interest and how to open a savings account. This is simple knowledge to remember. We then can learn the basic equations that are used to calculate the amount of interest earned on our money such as 4% on a $1000 investment over a year. Once we understand the formulas, we can apply them to other situations like investing more money at a higher interest rate. With that level of thinking, we can analyze how our investments might differ across other types of potential earnings like mutual funds or stocks. From that information, we can decide on what our best options might be. Ultimately, we could use all of this to develop a savings plan for ourselves or possibly use this knowledge in a financial advising career. Throughout this process, we are utilizing a higher order of thinking along the way.

In terms of breadth, Art Costas and Bena Kallick developed the Habits of Mind framework to help broaden our understanding of the different ways we think. The sixteen habits, when utilized appropriately and intentionally, have the capacity to affect decision-making and problem-solving in dramatic and beneficial ways. This is used widely in schools across the world to help learners have a deeper understanding of the diverse forms our thinking can take. Having a toolkit of strategies empowers us to recognize the needs of a situation and choose effective ways to address the task at hand.

Think of doing a research project. Throughout this work, we would be utilizing multiple habits of mind. We might start with questioning and posing problems. Then we would gather data through all of our senses. We may have to manage our impulsivity to stay focused on the project. As we compile the information, we apply past knowledge to this new situation. We get creative and innovative in searching for solutions. When finished with the work, we would need to be able to communicate our results with clarity and precision. This example highlights how our brains are using specific skills across the work. Being able to recognize and name what is going on in our thinking allows us to be more effective and intentional in whatever we are doing.

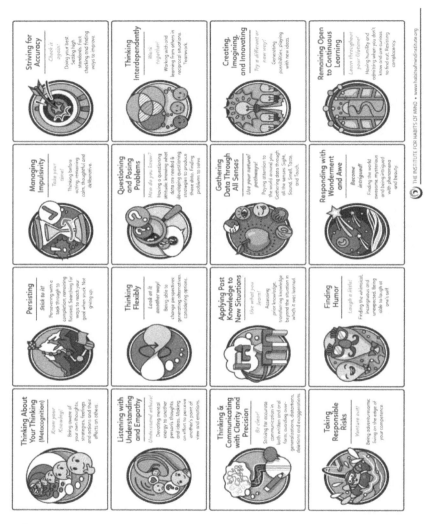

[8] "Hom 2021 Table (1)," The Institute for Habits of Mind, accessed April 6, 2023, https://www.habitsofmindinstitute.org/learning-the-habits/hom-2021-table-1/.

These theories on different perspectives of thinking help us visualize a structure around our mental processes. Gardner's work expands the context of how we define intelligence. We are smart in diverse ways, each of which empowers us to interact in the world around us differently and creatively. Bloom's work helps us see that thinking has levels of strength much like the gears of a car engine. Sometimes, we only need a little power to move forward. Other times, we must access the full strength of the system. Being able to identify what our range of mental capacity is and when to use the levels appropriately equips us to be better thinkers and problem-solvers. Costas and Kallick's work defines and clarifies the breadth of the strategies our brains can access to address any situation.

When we make the mental system visible through these different lenses, it enables us to have a deeper understanding of how our brain works. This empowers us to utilize our thinking more intentionally and effectively. Being able to name and access the elements of our thinking specifically and intentionally equips us for more successful decision-making.

The Shadow Side

As with all the strands, our mental component can be dysfunctional. Since thinking is a process instead of an absolute, we can develop ineffective and damaging mental patterns. Recognizing our faulty thinking and intentionally intervening in this process can help restore our alignment with our true selves.

As an example, consider this. Several years ago, illusionist David Copperfield made a jet disappear on live television. For all practical purposes, it looked like he was successful. At the heart of the act was the performer's ability to make the audience believe that what they were seeing was reality. Essentially, it's about convincing the minds of all those people that something that cannot be possible might have happened. The hard thing to swallow is that our minds are not that dependable sometimes.

Many of us struggle with how to handle our thoughts. In our minds, we can find ourselves wrestling with dark and destructive ideas that hijack our ability to function. It is helpful to remember that our minds are information processors not purveyors of truth. While we often forget, we actually have control over how we think about things. When we grasp that our brains are biological machines that can be conditioned and programmed in beneficial or detrimental ways, we gain access to changing our thought patterns. We can come to realize that much of our difficulties arise from cognitive distortions that we assume to be true. If we can break free from believing that everything we think is accurate and factual, we empower ourselves to develop healthier mental practices that lead to wholeness and balance.

Dealing with our mental health is a complex and broad arena that takes significant work and intention. Despite its difficulty, we can make huge strides toward our own well-being. Like any challenge, if we work on taking small steps toward the solution, we can make a difference. Seeing our minds and our thoughts for what they are is a starting point for developing healthy mental habits that support and encourage us in our daily lives. To do this work, we may need to ask for help in starting the process. Either way, putting our minds in proper perspective creates a solid foundation for us to move forward.

Back in my thirties, I was really struggling with anger issues that were greatly impacting my relationships and my work. I decided to go to a counselor to help me work through my situation. He introduced me to Cognitive Behavior Therapy and the work of David Burns, an American psychiatrist. This was the beginning of a shift in my life that has been ongoing for over twenty-five years. With the help of several other counselors and therapists, along with tremendous support from my wife, I have built a much stronger and healthier foundation for my mental health. The following material has made a substantial difference in my life.

Burns developed the concept of **cognitive distortions**. He introduced them in his book, *The Feeling Good Handbook* in the 1980s. His work further developed Cognitive Behavior Theory which was originally developed by Albert Ellis and Aaron Beck. The Mayo Clinic describes CBT as a therapy that helps you become aware of inaccurate or negative thinking so you can view challenging situations more clearly and respond to them in a more effective way.[9] Burns' checklist on the next page helps us truly articulate areas where our thinking is detrimental to our wellbeing.

---

[9] "Cognitive Behavioral Therapy," Mayo Clinic (Mayo Foundation for Medical Education and Research, March 16, 2019), https://www.mayoclinic.org/tests-procedures/cognitive-behavioral-therapy/about/pac-20384610.

Checklist of Cognitive Distortions[10]

1.	**All-or-nothing thinking**: You look at things in absolute, black-and-white categories.
2.	**Overgeneralization:** You view a negative event as a never-ending pattern of defeat.
3.	**Mental Filter:** You dwell on the negatives and ignore the positives.
4.	**Discounting the positives:** You insist that your accomplishments or positive qualities "don't count."
5.	**Jumping to conclusions:** (A) Mind reading - you assume that people are reacting negatively to you when there's no definite evidence for this; (B) Fortune Telling - you arbitrarily predict things will turn out badly.
6.	**Magnification or Minimization:** You blow things way out of proportion or you shrink their importance inappropriately.

---

[10] David D. Burns, M.D. Adapted from *Feeling Good: The New Mood Therapy*. New York: William Morrow & Company, 1980; Signet, 1981

7.	**Emotional Reasoning:** You reason from how you feel: "I feel like an idiot, so I really must be one." Or "I don't feel like doing this, so I'll put it off."
8.	**"Should Statements":** You criticize yourself or other people with "Shoulds" or "Shouldn'ts." "Musts," "Oughts," "Have tos" are similar offenders.
9.	**Labeling:** You identify with your shortcomings. Instead of saying, "I made a mistake," you tell yourself, "I'm a jerk," or "a fool," or "a loser."
10.	**Personalization and Blame:** You blame yourself for something you weren't entirely responsible for, or you blame other people and overlook ways that your own attitudes and behavior might contribute to a problem.

When my first counselor gave me this list, it was the beginning of a major change in my perspective on thinking. Just like when I got glasses in fourth grade and could finally see defined leaves on trees, having language and descriptions of what I was experiencing opened my eyes to new possibilities of how to deal with my emotional struggles. For example, I found that I was struggling with 3, 5, and 8 from the checklist. I was filtering everything through a negative lens and minimizing the positives in my life. I jumped to conclusions about what I thought other people were thinking and created whole stories around things that might not have even been true. The one I wrestled with the most was "shoulding" on myself. I was constantly criticizing myself on what I should have done or not done. Even to this day, I find myself falling back into these distorted thoughts.

Despite finding this life-changing information, it took nearly twenty years for me to fully internalize the power of this knowledge. As I came to embrace how my faulty thinking was impacting my life, I was empowered to find meaningful strategies to help resolve the problematic thinking and behavior. For instance, using the Ten Ways to Untwist Your Thinking, I found number 3, the Double Standard, to be helpful. When I realize that I would never speak to anyone else like I do to myself at times, I can reframe the situation with more self-compassion. Likewise, number 8, the Semantic method, helped me shift my "should" statements into less emotionally charged thoughts that focus on what I can learn from my mistakes and how I can improve in the future.

While it is possible to integrate these practices into our lives on our own, I and many others have found that having someone to guide us through this work and provide support through the process has led to greater success and integration into our daily lives. One of the healthiest and most intelligent things we can do is to ask for help.

TEN WAYS TO UNTWIST
YOUR THINKING[11]

1.	Identify the Distortion	Write down your negative thoughts so you can see which of the ten cognitive distortions you're involved in. This will make it easier to think about the problem in a more positive and realistic way.
2.	Examine the Evidence	Instead of assuming that your negative thought is true, examine the actual evidence for it. For example, if you feel that you never do anything right, you could list several things you have done successfully.
3.	The Double-Standard Method	Instead of putting yourself down in a harsh, condemning way, talk to yourself in the same compassionate way you would talk to a friend with a similar problem.
4.	The Experimental Technique	Do an experiment to test the validity of your negative thoughts. For example, if, during the episode of panic, you become terrified that you're about to die of a heart attack, you could jog or run up and down several flights of stairs. This will prove that your heart is healthy and strong.

---

[11] Ibid.

5.	Thinking in Shades of Grey	Although this method might sound drab, the effects can be illuminating. Instead of thinking about your problems in all-or-nothing extremes, evaluate things on a range of 0 to 100. When things don't work out as well as you hoped, think about the experience as a partial success rather than a complete failure. See what you can learn from the situation.
6.	The Survey Method	Ask people questions to find out if your thoughts and attitudes are realistic. For example, if you believe that public speaking anxiety is abnormal and shameful, ask several friends if they ever felt nervous before they gave a talk.
7.	Define Terms	When you label yourself "inferior" or "a fool" or "a loser," ask, "What is the definition of a 'fool'?" You will feel better when you see that there is no such thing as a "fool" or a "loser."
8.	The Semantic Method	Simply substitute language that is less colorful and emotionally loaded. This method is helpful for "should statements." Instead of telling yourself "I shouldn't have made that mistake," you can say, "It would be better if I hadn't made that mistake."
9.	Re-attribution	Instead of automatically assuming that you are "bad" and blaming yourself entirely for a problem, think about the many factors that may have contributed to it. Focus on solving the problem instead of

		using up all your energy blaming yourself and feeling guilty.
10.	**Cost-Benefit Analysis**	List the advantages and disadvantages of a feeling (like getting angry when your plane is late), a negative thought (like "No matter how hard I try, I always screw up"), or a behavior pattern (like overeating and lying around in bed when you're depressed). You can also use the Cost-Benefit Analysis to modify a self-defeating beliefs such as, "I must always try to be perfect."

Wrapping Up

Along the path of my mental health journey, I have moved from being completely unaware of how my mind works to having a meaningful outline of how the brain processes information. While my understanding is still incomplete, I have a stronger sense of mental balance than I have ever had. It has been important to me to explore how the brain receives and integrates data and experiences, what thinking dimensions look like across depth, breadth, and context, and how to identify and adjust dysfunctional thinking habits. When viewed through these lenses, we can better understand the form and function of how our brain works in processing information. This enables us to maximize our thinking power and minimize destructive thoughts that incapacitate us. For me, this has been a life-changing lesson to learn and implement in my life.

Activities

1. Take a Multiple Intelligence Assessment - https://personalitymax.com/multiple-intelligences-test/
2. Take the Habits of Mind Self-Assessment - https://www.habitsofmindinstitute.org/wp-content/uploads/2016/11/S8.5-Part4-Habits-of-Mind-self-assessment.pdf

EMOTIONAL

Growing up, dealing with emotions was rarely mentioned or emphasized. As far as I could tell, men only had three options of what they could feel: happy, angry, or none. Unfortunately, I didn't learn to process my anger as a child, and it carried over intensely into my adulthood. Like many others, I learned to wear a mask to hide my actual feelings. I conditioned myself to bury my anger, fear, frustrations, and grief until it became a volcano of emotions that erupted unexpectedly and often violently. Despite my dysfunction, or maybe because of it, I desired to understand what being emotionally balanced looks like. This led me to pursue becoming a school counselor. Despite my interest and focus, it has taken most of my life to finally have the vocabulary and skill set to process my emotions healthily and productively. Over these next sections, I want to share a framework and some meaningful habits that have helped me.

Studies have emerged showing the significance of emotions in every aspect of our lives. Being emotionally intelligent is not just a catch phrase, it is a critical strand in living a meaningful and healthy life. We have more resources now than ever before on how to process emotions purposefully and effectively. It is up to us to incorporate these into our daily lives and to teach these as the norms of a well-balanced life for all future generations. By doing so, we can truly equip ourselves to live fully and abundantly.

As mentioned in the introduction, our emotions are integrated into this sequence:

Experience: Some event or circumstance consciously registers in the brain.

Thought: Some series of preconceived ideas or thought processes begin to play out in the brain.

Feeling: The brain associates a feeling or physical reaction with the thought process.

Behavior: An action is chosen based on a reaction to the feeling.

Consequence: That action will have results that may or may not be beneficial.

Over the years, the steps of this sequence have generated different perspectives on emotions for me, influencing how I chose to deal with them effectively. Particularly, back in the late 1990s, I had the joy of being a school counselor for Bardstown High School. During that time, we began to host a senior retreat each year to allow students to explore various life skills that are necessary for a balanced and healthy life. In developing materials for the retreat, I came across the previously mentioned sequence as well as information about emotional intelligence and the significant impact it has on our lives. From these concepts, I developed a worksheet for the students to help them process emotions. There are four steps:

- Name it
- Claim it
- Embrace it
- Release it

Name It

First, we must be able to recognize and name the emotion we are feeling. Mark Brackett's book *Permission to Feel* is one of the best resources I have found to help with identifying and working with specific emotions. His Mood Meter app is a powerful tool to help articulate what we might be feeling. Essentially, if you cannot identify what you are feeling, it is difficult, if not impossible, to properly work through it. Likewise, Brené Brown's book, *Atlas of the Heart*, provides a comprehensive list and description of emotions. With these and other resources, we now have a much broader and clearer process for naming the diverse emotions we may be experiencing as well as what the root causes are that generate these feelings.

It is essential to understand that no emotion is bad in and of itself. Quite the contrary, each emotion is necessary and vital for strong human growth and development. The negativity of emotions comes from improper handling or purposeful misuse of emotions. So, naming our emotions, both pleasant and uncomfortable ones, is the place to start.

Claim It

The second step is to come to realize that only we are truly responsible for our emotions. We need to understand that our emotions are ours. Neuroscience shows that the connection between our thoughts and our emotions is a biological and chemical response to how we experience the world around us. If we are feeling something, it is due to our thought processes at work. Instead of blaming outside sources for our emotions, we need to own them. By doing so, we empower ourselves to address our emotions productively.

Embrace It

Third, emotions exist for a reason. We need to experience them. We are biologically wired to be emotional beings to help us exist. When we have an emotional response, we need to ask why we are feeling this. What is this emotion telling us? No matter what we are feeling, if we understand its purpose, we can learn to express it appropriately and meaningfully.

I chose the word *embrace* for several reasons. An emotion has a full life impact. It affects us physically, mentally, and spiritually as well. So, it is essential to completely engage with the feeling. Another way of visualizing this is to understand we must have a hold on something to be able to let go of it. By embracing the feeling, we can truly deal with it. Which emotion we are dealing with and to what degree we are feeling it determines the amount of work necessary to process the emotion.

For example, any loss will trigger a form of grief. The loss of a nice pen might only take a few minutes to get over but there could still be some emotion to process. On the other side of the spectrum, the loss of a spouse, parent, or child will affect us for a lifetime.

Some keys to effective processing are:

- **Awareness of the essentialness of time:** The intensity and depth of an emotion dictate the length of time for the body to work through. However, there is no exact timetable. We have to give ourselves space and grace to navigate through the process.
- **Realistic expectations:** So much of our struggle with emotions comes from unrealistic expectations of ourselves and others. We "should" ourselves into shame and blame. Taking a realistic and compassionate view of processing our emotions opens us up to be more effective in working through them.

- **Healthy thoughts and beliefs:** As mentioned in the prior section, working through cognitive distortions removes barriers so that we can see things more clearly which enables us to deal with our emotions.
- **Strong relationships:** Having safe and loving connections with others helps us create a support system where we can work through our emotions more successfully.

Release It

Last, we must learn to release emotions in healthy ways. Every feeling is temporary, but we are not always effective in letting them go. Unfortunately, due to how we minimize acceptance and discussion of our emotions, we tend to develop inappropriate and harmful ways to handle our feelings. Suppressing, masking, and ignoring our emotions often generate physical stress and pain throughout our bodies. By learning healthy ways to let go of our emotions, we create a clearer path to maintaining congruence.

Amelia and Emily Nagoski discuss in their book *Burnout: The Secret to Solving the Stress Cycle* that stress is a cycle with a beginning, middle, and ending. Until we complete the cycle, the chemical cocktail that comes from our emotional stress response is still in our bodies. This concept can be transferred to all emotions. Being intentional in processing feelings empowers us to move forward in positive ways. The Nagoski sisters suggest these seven ways to close the cycle:

- Physical Activity
- Breathing
- Positive Social Interaction
- Affection
- Crying
- Laughter

- Creative Expression

Each of these has had an impact on my life. Walking or playing disc golf are my go-to physical activities. A hug from my wife or children goes a long way to healing my soul. When it comes to creative expression, playing music, building furniture, or writing are powerful ways for me to complete the stress cycle.

Wrapping Up

Processing our emotions, naming, claiming, embracing, and releasing them enables us to appropriately internalize what they are telling us at any given moment. Whether we are infuriated at injustice, are deeply saddened at the loss of a loved one, or are overjoyed at the birth of a child, feeling these emotions help us bring meaning and understanding into our lives. When we accept the normalcy and necessity of experiencing our emotions fully, we free ourselves to be more congruent with our true selves.

Activities

1. Explore the MoodMeter app (Brackett)
2. Take an EQ test:
   https://positivepsychology.com/emotional-intelligence-tests/

SPIRITUAL

From an early age, church was a big part of my life. Like many others, I wanted to please my parents, Sunday school teachers, and pastors by trying to be a model example of a "good" boy. Over the years, I wrestled with what I was taught and what I was experiencing. While I still feel a deep connection to something bigger than myself, much of what I believed earlier in my life has changed. Working through my spiritual struggles has had a major impact on who I am today. Despite the pain and difficulty this journey has caused me, I am grateful for the life lessons those dilemmas have taught me.

I want to acknowledge that the spiritual strand of our lives may mean many different things to people. In this book, *spirituality* will center on the values and beliefs that guide our lives. This may include religion, but for our work, the two are not synonymous. We will focus on those deep core principles that we develop over time that provide the foundation for our choices and decisions in life.

One simple activity that really helped me focus on my values comes from Brené Brown's *Dare to Lead.*[12] Using a substantial list of values we all may consider important, readers are asked to pick their top ten. If values are missing that you find meaningful, add that to your list. Narrow your list to five. Then down to two (mine are love and balance). This exercise forces

---

[12] "Dare to Lead List of Values," Brené Brown, August 24, 2022, https://brenebrown.com/resources/dare-to-lead-list-of-values/.

us to home in on what we truly believe to be the most impactful in our lives.

These values emerge in our lives through our interactions with others, our life experiences, and our studies over time. They may change depending on various circumstances. However, at any given time, we have a set of beliefs, conscious or unconscious, that influence our daily lives. The more self-aware we become of what we believe, we strengthen our ability to live congruently with those values.

A major thread of our belief system is determining whether something is true or not. Truth is one of the most debated words in history. Each of us must wrestle with how we decide what is true and what is not. A scene from one of my favorite movies serves as a clarifier for me. The movie is *Contact*. It's based on the book by Carl Sagan and stars Jodie Foster and Matthew McConaughey. It's essentially about the human race making contact with intelligent beings from outer space. The connection comes from a radio signal, originally sent by us out into the universe, that is returned to Earth with an embedded blueprint that looks like the plans for intergalactic transport for a single person. So, with much more to the story, the machine is built but with an additional seat that is not in the sent plans. There is a dramatic scene late in the movie where Jodie's character, Ellie, is strapped into the added seat inside the capsule of the machine. During the launch, the seat begins vibrating uncontrollably. At this moment, Ellie sees a toy compass that she brought with her (more to that story as well) floating weightlessly out in front of her. She realizes that the man-made restraints were a mistake. So, she chooses to trust her intuition and releases herself from her restrictive chair, just before it collapses. This enables her to freely experience the intended purpose of the machine.

This particular scene has resonated with me for years. By not trusting the plan as it was originally sent, they added barriers and complications that were not necessary. Metaphorically, I extend this into my life as well. Truth is all around me. How I interact with it is up to me. I can seek to align with it humbly or stubbornly assume that I understand enough already. When I let go of trying to control everything and truly observe the patterns at work around me, I can glimpse a deeper process at work.

Truth doesn't depend on how we perceive it. Just because we believe something doesn't make it true. And not believing in something doesn't make it false. The more we try to grasp and hold to our limited and incomplete beliefs, the more truth slips through our fingers. Kind of like trying to hold water. Imagine tightening your grip on a handful of liquid; we minimize the amount we can hold. Instead, like our hands cupping water, if we open our minds and hearts to seek truth, we allow it to become more visible and approachable.

Every day, we get a chance to gather a little more information as to how life works. We continually have the opportunity to get curious about the things around us. However, as we become adults, and sometimes sooner, we begin to wall ourselves off from learning and growing for multiple reasons. We choose to hold onto a limited amount of knowledge and experience and declare it to be the absolute whole. But, just like Ellie in the movie, if we can break through the barriers of hindering ideas and attune to the realization that there is always more to learn, we can find a peaceful and meaningful connection to something much bigger than any of us. Are we willing to let go of our self-made boundaries to discover the truth in broader and more profound ways?

Moral Development

It may be helpful for understanding our spiritual dynamics to explore some models of moral development. From the work of Lawrence Kohlberg, Carol Gilligan, William Perry, and others, specific patterns emerge. Let's look at the basic principles of some of the theories.

Lawrence Kohlberg saw moral development across six stages focusing on social justice and rights[13].

Level 1 (Pre-Conventional)

1. Obedience and punishment orientation (How can I avoid punishment and pain?)
2. Self-interest orientation (What's in it for me?)

Level 2 (Conventional)

3. Interpersonal accord and conformity (How can I be a good boy/girl?)
4. Authority and social-order maintaining orientation (How do I live by law and order?)

Level 3 (Post-Conventional)

5. Social contract orientation (What is the common good?)
6. Universal ethical principles (How do I live by a universal code?)

According to Kohlberg, we start with a very egocentric mindset of "what do I gain" or "what pain will this cause me." We then move into a more structured set of beliefs based on our social and cultural conditioning, essentially the laws and regulations of society. From that legalistic foundation, some

---

[13] Kendra Cherry, "Levels of Developing Morality in Kohlberg's Theories," Verywell Mind (Verywell Mind, November 7, 2022), https://www.verywellmind.com/kohlbergs-theory-of-moral-development-2795071.

may choose to live by a set of personalized values that they have proven over time and experience.

Carol Gilligan was a research assistant under Kohlberg. She came to believe his work focused only on a male point of view. She took his ideas and framed them through a feministic lens focusing on relationships, care, and responsibility.

Moral position	Definition of what is morally good
Position 1: Survival orientation	Action that considers one's personal needs only
Position 2: Conventional care	Action that considers others' needs or preferences, but not one's own
Position 3: Integrated care	Action that attempts to coordinate one's own personal needs with those of others

Both Kohlberg and Gilligan give us a framework for spiritual growth that clearly shows movement toward an interdependent and intrinsic life. Moving from a self-centered mindset to a balanced belief system that is centered on being mutually beneficial, we enhance our relationships with others and ourselves.

One other theory that can inform our spiritual development is William Perry's Scheme of Ethical Development. His work emerged from working with college students and observing the evolution of their thinking as they encountered broader world perspectives. Perry's work helps us see a pathway toward an open and more compassionate worldview. When we move from a rigid right or wrong mentality toward a curious, thoughtful, and receptive mindset, we allow ourselves to see others as human beings just like us who are trying to make sense of the world from where they stand.[14]

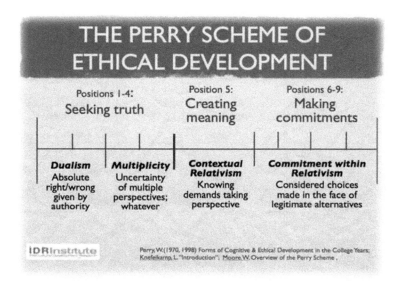

It is important to note that these theories are incomplete in their scope because they are developed with a specific focus, creating a narrower lens on our human experience. Likewise, an additional flaw in development theories, in general, is the oversimplification of major transitions into linear stages. The process of growth is nonlinear. People can move in and out of these stages in different aspects of their lives and at various

---

[14] "Overview of Perry Scheme," The Perry Network, 2013, http://perrynetwork.org/?page_id=2.

ages. However, analyzing these models can still give us meaningful insight into our spiritual development.

When we look at these frameworks, some common threads across them suggest a process at work. For instance, each of these models reveals movement from a narrow, self-centered mindset into a more outwardly focused, broader worldview. Amid this flow, they suggest we must transition into a legalistic and structured belief system first before we can reach a higher level of moral reasoning. The eventual outcome for each is a personally chosen, internalized worldview that emerges from the lived experiences of the individual.

It helps me to frame this process in a cyclical set of stages:

- **Initial:** we start with a blank slate
- **Adopted:** we assume others' beliefs
- **Wrestling:** we encounter and struggle with doubts and uncertainties
- **Integrated:** we internalize personalized beliefs forged by experience and reflection

We start as an open book, taking in all that is around us from our family, our community, and our culture. For much of our early life, we are just sponges that absorb much of what we observe and hear. In time, we assume some of the beliefs and values of others. As we explore and integrate these "external" views, we come to gaps and possible contradictions in them. This leads us to the "wrestling" stage. In this stage, we must confront the possibility that something we believed prior may not be accurate or true. This incongruence can be very unsettling and sometimes painful. Until we resolve these contradictions, we can be stuck in this stage for a substantial amount of time.

Kazimierz Dąbrowski, a Polish psychiatrist calls the "wrestling" stage **positive disintegration**. His work focused on similar transitions as Perry's but emphasizes that not everyone will move through the stages. With the stress and anxiety that these transitions produce, he proposed that many choose to stay fixed in an incomplete stage. He worked to help others to see that unless some things "disintegrate," more healthy and meaningful perspectives cannot emerge. By accepting the unraveling or collapse of immature beliefs, the process, despite the pain and uncertainty, inevitably produces a positive result.

From our struggles and examination of the wrestling stage, a belief system can emerge that is congruent with our experiences and perspective. This is where we integrate our beliefs into our daily routines. We react from a firmer foundation that can give us a sense of stability and purpose.

Integration is more a continual process than a destination. We move through a series of iterations of learning and letting go, learning and letting go. T. S. Eliot spoke to this:

We shall not cease from exploration, and the end of all our exploring will be to arrive where we started and know the place for the first time.[15]

A Butterfly Metaphor

This process reminds me of the transition a caterpillar goes through to become a butterfly. When a caterpillar hatches from its egg, it immediately begins to eat. And eat, and eat, and eat. Essentially it eats its whole surroundings (similar to my children). For the first stages of its life, it essentially just consumes and grows, becoming a larger and larger caterpillar. I imagine at some point, it begins to wonder if that is all there is, simply eating and getting bigger. Something shifts and a deep calling pushes it to look inward. A transformation begins. Taking on a new direction and form, it isolates itself in a

---

[15] T.S. Eliot, "Little Gidding," *Four Quartets.* 1942.

chrysalis. It is at this point that the complete disintegration of the prior life takes place. In my mind, I imagine that it is a lonely and scary phase for the caterpillar. Yet, in time, a metamorphosis occurs; an awakening of its true self begins.

The next phase is a challenging one as well. With its new sense of purpose and direction, it must shed its prior life. It is no easy task. The process requires it to bite a small hole in its chrysalis and slowly squeeze itself out. This appears to be a painful and stressful journey. There have been some observers who felt that they would help the process along by cutting open the chrysalis to speed up the process. This produces a misshapen creature with undeveloped wings which sadly dies soon thereafter. So, it is a necessity for the caterpillar to endure the pressure and strain of struggling through its constraints so that the fluids in its body will move into the budding wings and allow them to take full form. Then and only then, can the transformation be completed. What started out as essentially a worm emerges as one of the most beautiful things on earth.

In many ways, our spiritual development is like this phenomenon. Where are we in the cycle? Are we in the early stage of growth where we are more egocentric? Just trying to see what we can consume? Or have we begun the chrysalis phase where we are wrestling with the essential questions of who we are? Have we begun the hard work of releasing our wings? This process of change is ongoing in each of us. We need to allow the trials and tribulations as well as the joys and victories to teach us and guide us into the full discovery of who we are and what we have to offer. When we do, this incredible metamorphosis of becoming our true selves gives us meaning and purpose. We are meant to fly! We are meant to bring beauty to the world around us!

Another aspect of the spiritual strand of our lives is the question of whether we are part of something bigger than ourselves. For many of us, we are drawn to the mysteries of the universe and our place in them. We try to come to some understanding of the currents at work all around us. Science seeks to answer many of these questions. Religion does as well. The powerful interaction between faith and fact has led the human race to multiple points of view. A significant measure of this is that there are over 4,000 distinct religions on the planet[16]. As part of our moral development, we must sift through all the diverse thoughts we encounter. While the challenge is daunting at times, if we can approach this work with an open mind and heart, we are able to discern what resonates with us and what doesn't. The biggest obstacle is listening to the "still, small voice" within us when the cultural expectations are noisily grabbing our attention.

One of my practices in searching for truth is to look at how the systems of nature function. For instance, the human body is a marvelous and mysterious dynamic operation. It has an amazing system to heal wounds and injuries. I won't pretend to fully understand how everything works, but here are a few things I have learned. When we get a cut, the body immediately responds by sending a variety of types of cells to stop the bleeding and fight infection. An unseen communication system tells the surrounding tissues to work together to build replacement parts for the damaged area. While it takes time, when the body is healthy and active, the process works incredibly well.

It is the same way with humans collectively. When we are at our best, people respond rapidly to help each other during difficult situations such as accidents, sickness, natural disasters, or the loss of loved ones. In those moments, we feel called to

---

[16] Stephen Juan, "What Are the Most Widely Practiced Religions of the World?," The Register® - Biting the hand that feeds IT (The Register, December 7, 2018),
https://www.theregister.com/2006/10/06/the_odd_body_religion/.

step up with the skills and resources that we can provide. We feel a greater sense of purpose from doing so.

Extending the parallel a bit further, there are underlying forces at work that are guiding the body and the world itself. We can ignore them and even fight them with ignorant and destructive behavior. However, when we are attuned to the beneficial systems operating around us, we empower our bodies to maintain a healthy balance. This enables us to be ready to respond to others as needed at any given moment. When we do this, we find a pathway to meaningful and joyful lives.

One other metaphor really speaks to me. While in college, I took several chemistry classes. One of my favorite instruments to work with was a crucible. Essentially, crucibles are used to heat things to extreme temperatures to discover aspects of the compound being observed. In the case of raw ores, the heat begins to break down the structure of the sample and helps separate the true metal from any impurities that have clustered around it. When the proper temperatures are reached, it is possible to skim off the unwanted material and be left with the pure element.

Life has a way of acting like a crucible. The stress and strain of all the uncertainty, the losses, and the changes in our lives reveal varying aspects of our inner qualities. At times we feel like we are breaking or melting down. The lesson of the crucible is that what feels like a destructive process is actually a path to refinement. It is critical oftentimes for us to go through the "fire" to reveal the non-essential material that is in the way of us being our true selves. Crises, as hard as they may be, are substantial ways of helping us to see what we may need to remove from our lives so that we can move toward wholeness and balance.

The questions arise, do we want to? Are we willing to take a hard look at the things in our lives that are hindering us from living to our full potential? Much like gold and silver ore, within each of us is something precious and valuable. Being in the crucible can be a traumatic experience, but the intense process can help us become the beautiful and valuable people we are meant to be. Through this lens, we can view this difficult and trying time as an opportunity for meaningful personal growth and discovery.

Wrapping Up

Ultimately, our spiritual foundation comes down to faith. Again, faith is a word that means very different things to many people. While I am a mathematician and a scientist by training, I am also a person of faith. I don't see this as a contradiction. Instead, I see the two as essentially the same. Every discipline can be boiled down to a set of assumptions. At some point, you must choose to accept something that cannot be fully proven. Isn't that faith? Over my lifetime, my perceptions of faith have changed, evolved, or emerged. One thing I am sure of is that each of us must choose what we believe. Learning from each other can help sharpen our values and worldview; however, no one has the right to dictate what we believe. Whatever we decide to believe, it is helpful to remember that spiritual growth is a journey, not a destination.

Activities

1. Take an Enneagram assessment. There are many to choose from. Here is one example: https://www.truity.com/test/enneagram-personality-test)

2. Do Brené Brown's Value Exercise: https://brenebrown.com/resources/dare-to-lead-list-of-values/

Bringing it Back Together

While there is great value in assessing each strand separately, each is inextricably interconnected with the others. Just like the stool, the whole piece is completely dependent on the stability and strength of each leg. Whatever impacts one will affect them all, like the way we struggle with our mental health when we are physically sick. Mind, body, heart, and soul work in conjunction with each other to provide the framework for who we are.

The image below is a mental model that helps me visualize all of this holistically. At the center of it, all is our true self. Extending from that core are our four strands. The strength and healthiness of each of them provide the support structure for our outer self, the part that those around us see. When our true selves and our outer selves are not congruent, we will be out of balance and dysfunctional. Usually, that means that one or more of the strands needs attention and restoration. I imagine this as deflated tire. With direct attention, time, and energy, our balance can be restored.

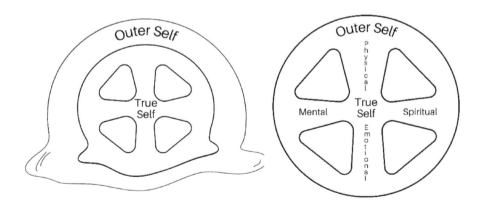

One of the most influential tools that I have found to help assess my life and empower me to make the necessary changes to live in congruence is Brené Brown's guideposts for wholehearted living. In her book, *The Gifts of Imperfection*, she uses the guideposts to comprehensively describe what the characteristics of a healthy balanced life look like and what factors adversely affect them.

She has created a sliding scale for each guidepost which provides a structure and vocabulary to define a more purposeful and balanced life. Her research on vulnerability, shame, relationships, and leadership has created a pathway for many to assess, evaluate, and reform the way they understand themselves and others.

Her ten guideposts are:

1. Cultivating Authenticity and Letting Go of What Other People Think
2. Cultivating Self-Compassion and Letting Go of Perfectionism
3. Cultivating Your Resilient Spirit and Letting Go of Numbing and Powerlessness
4. Cultivating Gratitude and Joy and Letting go of Scarcity and Fear of the Dark
5. Cultivating Intuition and Trusting Faith and Letting Go of the Need for Certainty
6. Cultivating Creativity and Letting Go of Comparison
7. Cultivating Play and Rest and Letting Go of Exhaustion as a Status Symbol and Productivity as Self-Worth
8. Cultivating Calm and Stillness and Letting Go of Anxiety as a Lifestyle
9. Cultivating Meaningful Work and Letting Go of Self-Doubt and Supposed-To
10. Cultivating Laughter, Song, and Dance. And Letting Go of Cool and Always in Control

10 Guideposts for Wholehearted Living

FROM BRENÉ BROWN'S "THE GIFTS OF IMPERFECTION"

Letting go of...	Cultivating...
WHAT PEOPLE THINK	AUTHENTICITY
PERFECTIONISM	SELF-COMPASSION
NUMBING AND POWERLESSNESS	A RESILIENT SPIRIT
SCARCITY AND FEAR OF THE DARK	GRATITUDE & JOY
NEED FOR CERTAINTY	INTUITION & TRUSTING FAITH
COMPARISON	CREATIVITY
EXHAUSTION AS A STATUS SYMBOL AND PRODUCTIVITY AS SELF-WORTH	REST & PLAY
ANXIETY AS A LIFESTYLE	CALM & STILLNESS
SELF-DOUBT & "SUPPOSED TO"	MEANINGFUL WORK
COOL AND "ALWAYS IN CONTROL"	LAUGHTER, SONG & DANCE

ILLUSTRATED BY AVALON MCKENZIE

During a particularly difficult time in my life, I was able to see myself across many of these guideposts which helped me identify areas of growth. With support from my family, my counselor, and others, I began the work of moving toward a more congruent life that allowed me to live fully with my integrity. You may want to take the Wholehearted Inventory at https://brenebrown.com/wholeheartedinventory/ as a good starting point.

As I mentioned before, I struggled with thoughts of not being enough, of not being worthy unless I was perfect or pleasing everyone, and of a sense of resignation that it could never be any better. This internal conflict generated a wide range of anxiety at different times throughout my life. In hindsight, I can now see how I was numbing myself in numerous ways to avoid the pain and hurt of my perceived unworthiness. I was pulling away from people that I loved and building walls around me to unsuccessfully escape my discomfort and pain.

By taking an honest look at my life and accepting the state of my thoughts and behaviors, I was able to begin the work of restoration and healing. It is still an ongoing journey, but I am putting effective habits in place that are helping me sustain a congruent life. By living within my integrity, I have found that my relationships, my work, and my daily life are more meaningful and joyful. In Part II, we will focus on how to take congruency in our individual lives and use it to give ourselves away in ways that allow us to live abundantly.

Part II:

Giving Ourselves Away

Interdependence

Throughout Part I, we have been exploring how to find and accept ourselves. In the framework of EQ, we have been examining ways to become more self-aware and to self-manage more effectively. The result of this process is to become more congruent with our true selves. This implies a level of independence from anything that stands in the way of us living with our integrity.

However, independence is not the end goal. We are hard-wired to work interdependently with each other. To paraphrase John Donne, no person is an island. We find fulfillment and purpose when we use our talents, skills, and experiences to serve others. Mahatma Gandhi put it this way, "The best way to find yourself is to lose yourself in the service of others." This quote is the foundation for the last part of the theme statement of this book: Give ourselves away.

So, what does this look like across the different areas of our lives? In this section, we will focus on how giving ourselves away enables us to have meaningful relationships, purposeful work, and enriching lives.

RELATIONSHIPS

Relationships are the most important things in our lives, and, sometimes the most complicated. At my age, I have experienced the full range of relationships. My wife and I have been married since 1986. Our children were born in 1989, 1992, and 1995. I have two brothers, a sister, eighteen aunts and uncles, more than forty cousins, and so on. I have taught or worked with over 6,000 students and staff throughout my career as well as interacted with hundreds more through church, sports, or other community events. In all these connections, I have experienced great joy and tremendous pain, meaningful interactions and major divisions, long-lasting friendships, and uncomfortable acquaintances. I say all of this to emphasize that despite this multitude of relationships, I am still learning what it means to truly understand and fully engage with others. However, there have been some major takeaways throughout the years. In the following pages, we will explore the diverse relationships we can have and how we can create more meaningful ones in the process.

First off, for me, the core of every relationship is love. Unfortunately, the word love often loses its meaning in the multiple ways it is used in our language. Some see it as an emotion; others speak of it as a spiritual dynamic. Some refer to it as an act of will while others see it as a state of being. So, to bring some clarity for the purposes of this book, I define love to be *a commitment to the good of the other.*

Let's focus on three words in this definition: *commitment*, *good*, and *other*. *Commitment* is an action. It is a choice. When we commit to something, we are giving our attention, resources, and energy to it. We choose to dedicate ourselves to a person, a group, or a cause fully. The word *good* is another one that can have diverse meanings. For this definition, it is a noun representing anything that benefits, enriches, or empowers in a healthy, integral way. *Other* refers to the recipient of the intention. It encompasses anyone we interact with—including ourselves. So, being committed to the good of the other can show up in an infinite number of ways. Maybe it is feeding someone or folding laundry. Holding hands or giving a hug. Guiding a child or holding people accountable. We can reframe almost any daily behavior into an act of love if the intention is to bring about good in the life of others. So, let's dive deeper into how love impacts relationships with ourselves, family and friends, life partners, and the world around us.

With Self

Put your oxygen mask on first... If you have been on a plane, you will have heard this instruction in case of cabin depressurization. It has become the signature phrase for self-compassion. In many aspects of our culture, we are asked to minimize ourselves in contrast to others. However, I find it interesting that the Bible reference about loving others has an additional clause - "as yourself." I interpret that to mean that you can only love others to the depth that you love yourself. Again, in the context of the early definition of love, loving ourselves is being committed to our own good.

In the first part of the book, we explored the foundation for self-care and aligning with our true selves. We must maintain our physical, mental, emotional, and spiritual health to be able to contribute to others regularly. To put it boldly, we cannot have long-term, meaningful relationships with others until we deeply connect with our true selves and learn to nurture our own holistic health. Likewise, taking care of ourselves first is not a selfish thing as long as we are preparing ourselves to serve others more effectively and efficiently. You cannot give others something you don't have to give.

The need for self-love can reveal itself in many ways. A while back, I was heading out to take one of our cars for service. About four miles into my trip, it dawned on me that I was driving our other car. Realizing my mistake, I stopped and sheepishly turned around to go and get the right vehicle. I suppose I could have stubbornly kept driving to my destination, but it would have cost me more time, caused me more headache, and would have taken me farther from successfully accomplishing my goal. As ludicrous as that sounds, I have lived that way with many choices in my life. Instead of acknowledging and accepting that I had made mistakes in decisions or actions, I doubled down in the wrong direction and made things far worse.

At the root of many of my past struggles is the dysfunctional belief that my worth was dependent on being perfect or pleasing others. So, I often continued going in the wrong direction just so I didn't have to face my perceived unworthiness. I have learned and continue to learn now that my value as a person is an inherent quality, not something I have to earn. And when I make mistakes or fail at some tasks, it is an integral part of being human. It is not an indictment of my worth; it is just an opportunity to learn and grow.

Sometimes we can become aware of our errant directions on our own. However, more often than not, we may need help and perspective from others. It might take a doctor, a counselor, a family member, a close friend, or occasionally, a stranger that crosses our path, to give us insight into things previously unseen. While it can be uncomfortable or even painful to realize that we are going down the wrong path, the sooner we can make the necessary corrections, the sooner we can get back on track toward living a meaningful and successful life. In a profound way, this is one of the greatest acts of self-compassion we can do.

With Life Partners

Over the years of working with students, I would often shift to my counselor hat instead of my math teacher one. During a conversation with my class about dating and establishing meaningful relationships, a novel idea came to mind. I asked them to imagine letting someone who is congruent with their integrity having a value of 1, represented by a complete circle.

Then, let someone who is not fully aligned with their true self be a fraction, such as ½, represented by a partially deflated circle.

In this context, it dawned on me that relationships are multiplication-based, not addition. Two people who are in a room together are addition.

$$1+1=2.$$

That situation doesn't necessarily generate a relationship. However, when two people fully interact with each other, it is more like

$$1 \times 1 = 1.$$

Two separate people can create one relationship, but it requires intentionality. For ease of writing and referencing, we will call this the Universal Principle of Relationships (UPR).

Over the years, this concept has evolved in a few interesting ways. In the movie Jerry McGuire, Renee Zellweger tells Tom Cruise, "You complete me!" While this is a sweet sentiment, it is not true. We can only find wholeness and balance within ourselves. We can use the UPR to represent this. When two people are struggling to find themselves, they may believe that they can find completeness with each other. This is "addition" thinking:

$$\frac{1}{2} + \frac{1}{2} = 1$$

However, by applying the multiplication rule, we get:

$$\frac{1}{2} \times \frac{1}{2} = \frac{1}{4}$$

This emphasizes that a relationship that is based on incongruence can lead to having less than what we had originally. The only way to have a full and complete relationship is for both people to be whole:

$$1 \times 1 = 1.$$

While this may seem to trivialize one of the most important elements of our lives, in its simplicity, it shows a pathway for building a meaningful life with a partner.

That early discussion evolved into a mini course that I would teach to students called Relationships 101. From these sessions, we developed some Laws of Love:

1. The UPR 1x1=1 (see above)

2. Find your path first, then see who is walking along with you.

   From my personal experience and that of many others, in our attempt to find someone to complete us while we are incomplete in ourselves, we often connect with others doing the same, creating that minimal relationship. If we take the time to find ourselves and develop our sense of purpose first, we will be more attuned to others around us who would be meaningful partners on the journey.

3. Practice friendship first:

   Due to our biological wiring, we are prone to rush into the physical aspects of relationships. While this is normal, we would be better off developing our connections mentally, emotionally, and spiritually as deeply as the physical. These are the elements of friendship that will sustain any relationship over time.

4. Every successful relationship includes these elements of love:
   - **Unconditional acceptance** – of the person, but not necessarily their actions. Seeing each other as always worthy of love but working to eliminate detrimental behaviors.
   - **Realistic expectations** – setting clear intentions, clarifying expectations, and acknowledging differences to reduce disappointments and frustrations.
   - **Gratitude** – the purposeful appreciation of and for one another, expressed through daily words and

actions. Feeling a warm gratefulness for all efforts, big or small.

- **Empathy-** internalizing and reacting to others with a deep understanding of what they are feeling.
- **Honest and open communication** – one of the hardest elements of any relationship, but one of the most crucial. It takes consistent, intentional work in creating a safe space to be vulnerable with each other. Doing so can be challenging at times, but the impact on a relationship can be transformative.
- **Trust** – the cornerstone and foundation for any meaningful relationship. Built into this are honesty, integrity, accountability, and dependability. This reveals itself in the comfort of knowing that your partner sees you, values you, and will show up for you in the ways you need them to.

Creating a healthy and meaningful partnership takes substantial work. One of the best resources I have encountered is the work of John and Julia Gottman through the Gottman Institute. With over four decades of research and intense investigation into the dynamics of successful and dysfunctional relationships, they have identified clear guidelines that can positively impact any long-term commitment. These seven habits have been proven to strengthen and enhance relationships[17]:

1. **Share Love Maps**: Getting to know each other in terms of what we like or need. Gary Chapman speaks to this idea by identifying our love languages.

---

[17] John Gottman, *The Seven Principles of Making Marriage Work: A Practical Guide from the Country's Foremost Relationship Expert* (New York, NY: Three Rivers Press, 1999).

2. **Nurture Your Fondness & Admiration**: Intentionally showing we care about the other person by focusing on and acknowledging the positives.

3. **Turn Towards Each Other Instead of Away**: When our partner bids for our attention, we make a conscious effort to engage with each other.

4. **Let Your Partner Influence You**: The key word is *partner*. Seeing each other as equals and valuing the other's point of view and opinions empowers equitable decision-making.

5. **Solve Your Solvable Problems**: Take the steps to address problems that can be resolved with common resolve and dedication to the relationship above all else.

6. **Overcome Gridlock**: This does not necessarily mean fixing problems but taking steps to overcome them by acknowledging them and reframing them in a meaningful way.

7. **Create Shared Meaning**: Building connection and common experiences every day in the midst of the routine and demands of daily life allows us to create a life story that celebrates each other and highlights the little joys and accomplishments along the way. By stitching together meaningful and special moments, we create a quilt of a beautiful life.

Wrapping Up

Having a meaningful long-term relationship with a partner requires that we find ourselves first, then see who is walking along with us. We cannot always be fully whole; however, trying to have someone else complete us will lead to dysfunction. When we lovingly seek to meet each other's needs, hold space for each other through times of growth, and work daily to see, hear, and value each other, we create a strong foundation for a phenomenal relationship.

Activities

1. Take Gary Chapman's 5 Love Languages quiz https://5lovelanguages.com/quizzes/love-language
2. Read the Gottman's *The Love Prescription* and do the seven-day experiment.

With Family

We don't get to choose into which family we are born. Some are loving and supportive most of the time, while others are dysfunctional and detrimental due to multiple reasons. Yet, no matter what the circumstances are, we are bonded to our family in many ways. Our parents lay the foundation for the world we come to know. If we have siblings, they help create the parameters that guide our lives. Extended family such as aunts, uncles, and cousins can provide diversity and depth to our journey. As we come to know ourselves, we will find that we are greatly influenced by this network of people around us.

To have meaningful relationships with our parents, siblings, or others, we must intentionally create space and time to build connections and encourage each other's growth. The difficulty lies in being willing to accept that despite our genetic similarities, we can be wildly different individuals who are trying to figure out our place in this world. Our expectations for family are often far more unrealistic than what we would have for others outside our crew. This sets us up for hurt, disappointment, and conflict as each of us tries to find our true selves.

By incorporating the elements of love mentioned earlier we can overcome the obstacles that family relationships can develop. If we are intentional in accepting each other unconditionally and having realistic expectations of each other, we can make a psychologically safe space to better understand each other. With a heart of gratitude and love, we can come to see each other fully and value the inherent worth of one another.

As an example, take my father and me. We have a complicated relationship. We see the world very differently. We can butt heads with the best of them over multiple things going on in the world. If we were to let things get too heated, we might never talk to each other again. But we are intent on focusing on the things that bring us together. We can talk for days about college basketball, our fishing trips, the crazy weather, and various places we have been in the US. The key to this is that we have a relationship that we want to maintain. We must work hard at it because we have some drastically different values in a few areas. These hot topics can be divisive, but we choose to approach them with a spirit of civility and mutual respect. It is still difficult at times and my temper can flare up in a heartbeat when he says something contrary to my beliefs. But the point once again is that I love my dad despite our differences and am willing to find a better path for our relationship.

If we end up having children of our own, we will experience the other side of the coin. Being responsible for another human being changes our lives in profound ways. Helping them to discover who they are adds multiple layers of complexity over the years. Yet, despite the significant challenge of raising a child, it can be one of the most rewarding dynamics of our lives.

I heard many years ago that two of the most important things to give our kids are roots and wings. The "roots" part develops over time. Sometimes it is intentional, but mostly these are the things that they learn by watching us. This slow and steady process is practically invisible while they are growing up. In hindsight, I wish I had better understood what they were internalizing; I would have done some things differently for sure.

The "wings" side of this process can come suddenly and intensely. When they leave as young adults for any number of reasons, we must come to terms that our kids are not our possessions. We have simply been the guardians and providers preparing them to leave the nest. Letting them go to find their way in the world is exhilarating and overwhelming at the same time.

My kids are living their own lives now. I have come to realize that the "wings" dynamic never really stops. They are constantly flying off on new opportunities. That same mixture of emotions still stirs within me whenever they choose a new path or stage in their journeys. I am thankful that I still feel this swirl of feelings because it signifies that our bond is still real and meaningful.

When I was a young adult, I was oblivious to how my parents felt when I rushed out to try my wings. I couldn't wait to find my place in this world. Knowing what I know now, I am grateful for the foundation and the freedom my folks gave me as I stepped out into adulthood. Being on the parent side now, I can deeply appreciate what my mom and dad went through.

As my wife and I have watched our children grow into adults, we have experienced the full gamut of emotions on this amazing journey. We are proud of who they are and what they are doing with their lives. We look forward to having them visit us whenever they can. However, we know that for them to truly find purpose and meaning in their lives, they must fly away.

With Friends

A while back I was talking to a colleague with whom I had worked for over six years. We were both starting new paths and would be going our separate ways. Toward the end of our conversation, we both committed to trying to stay in touch going forward. Our intentions are good, but, at least in my case, I am terrible at keeping those connections. Over my career, I have worked in at least 11 different places and interacted with thousands of amazing people. At each of these schools or offices, I grew to love and value colleagues like family. In the midst of the work with these teams or groups, we created relationships that were meaningful and significant. Much of who I am today was forged through those relationships.

However, in each situation, within a few weeks of moving away, I began to lose touch with them. Despite how important these people were to me; time and distance eroded the immediacy of those relationships.

Neuroscience and psychology can help explain why these connections tend to fade over time. Research shows that, at our best, we can only really focus on three to five things at a time. Unless something is in our immediate path of activity, it is unlikely to be an integral part of our thinking. As we are in the flow of our day, we go through thousands of iterations of addressing the needs and demands of the moment. The people we see every day get the advantage of being involved in this process and therefore stay in our minds more often. Additionally, there is evidence that we can only maintain active relationships with around 150 people. So, with every new phase of our lives, we expand our circle of interactions. Depending on the situation and length of time, we can surpass the 150 mark quickly. We then must prioritize our connections so that we can function effectively.

As I write this, it all sounds cold and sterile. It seems to minimize the heart of our relationships. So, how do we find balance between the systemic process at work and the emotional dynamics we experience? For me, I have come to realize that just because certain people haven't crossed my mind lately or I haven't crossed theirs, it doesn't have to take away from the specialness of our past relationships. It seems to be the default mode for most of us to paint every unknown situation with a negative brush. The truth is despite the lack of direct connection with our previous friends, the spark of love and affection is still there for each other. Recognizing this fact and knowing the science of how the mind works, we can embrace that they are just living their lives the best they can within the limits of human nature. So, we can choose to be grateful for the time we had with them and how they impacted our lives. And, when they cross our minds, we can reach out to them occasionally. If nothing else, we can smile and remember them fondly.

Given the process at work in our brains and the impermanence of all things, it is a reminder that we need to be more present with those around us daily. There's an old saying I heard growing up: Love 'em while you got 'em. We would all benefit from taking a moment to appreciate those around us now and say a word of thanks to those from our past.

With the World

Fundamentally, every human is the same. We are biological animals interacting with the planet, developing physically, mentally, emotionally, and spiritually during the time we exist. However, every person's experience is unique. It's all about context. Nothing has meaning except in context. For the most part, we don't get to choose our context for much of our lives. How would each of our lives have been different if we were born on the other side of the world?

In my life, I have traveled to multiple countries, have met a wide variety of people, and have studied their many cultures, beliefs, and practices. While there are some beliefs and actions that I oppose and much that I don't understand, I have never met a person that was not worthy of being loved and respected. Every time I have shared a meal with someone, listened to their story, and walked a little bit along their path, I have gained a new perspective and a broader understanding.

While I would like to think that I have been inclusive in my work and relationships over the years, I have actually had a life-long struggle with my own internal biases and prejudices. If we are really honest with ourselves, we all have wrestled with some kind of "ism" – racism, sexism, heterosexism, ageism, classism, and so on. We have all minimized groups of people at times and in some ways. We have drawn lines, dividing us against them. We have developed our own implicit biases, creating blind spots in how we interact with the world. If we are going to make meaningful changes in addressing this struggle, we must start with ourselves.

As an educator since 1985, I have had the pleasure of working with students from all walks of life. Throughout these years, I believed that I was an advocate and ally in the fight against the "isms." However, over the past several years I have become aware of some of my blind spots. A series of events helped open my eyes to dynamics at work in my thoughts and behaviors. The first revelation came when I was introduced to the Implicit Association Test (IAT) through my training to become a leadership and life coach.

We were asked to take the IAT on racism as part of an evening assignment. Although at the time, I had never heard of Project Implicit, I have since found it to be a life-changing experience. Anthony Greenwald and Mahzarin Banaji began a research project at Harvard in 1995 that is ongoing today. They created a neuroscience-based way to assess our underlying implicit biases toward multiple groups, concepts, and ideologies. Taking the race test, I became aware that I had an automatic racial preference for White relative to Black. While it was deemed a "slight" preference rather than "moderate" or "strong," I still was moved to rethink how I "showed up" in my relationships with people of color. I went on to take a few more of the fifteen different assessments. These revealed different aspects of underlying biases toward gender, sexuality, religion, and other factors. This awakening pushed me to reflect much more intently on how I truly interacted with others around me.

From my experience with the IAT, I began to search for articles and books that might help me become more aware of my conscious and unconscious beliefs. During this same timeframe, the murders of George Floyd and Breonna Taylor fueled an intense public dialogue on how systemic racism was deeply intertwined in so much of our daily lives. In this context, I came across Ibram X Kendi's book, *How to Be an Antiracist*. For the first time in my life, I found language and insight that helped me articulate elements of my personal worldview. Specifically, I came to understand that for much of my life, I have been an assimilationist. While I was truly fighting against racism that saw others as less than and inferior, I was blind to the fact that I continually used my white-male-middle-class-heterosexuality as the standard to which everyone should aspire. While I believed everyone could equally attain my same level, I failed to understand that I still centered the world around my personal set of values. Kendi's work helped me to see that to be truly antiracist, I needed to internalize that all people are truly worthy as they are and that other perspectives, languages, and experiences are every bit as important as my own. This expands out to all of the "isms" we face.

Try to visualize the world around us as a set of concentric circles outward from us. There would be a group of people in each circle that represent the depth of the relationship that we have. Our families would be in the closest circle. Our close friends and colleagues in the next. Our neighbors may be next. And so on. Ultimately, we can include the whole world in a very large circle. As we move out  through the rings, we are faced with decisions on whether we are going to choose to love this group or build a wall to separate ourselves from them. What group or groups are beyond building a relationship with? If we choose the wall and say it's us versus them, we take a step toward conflict and harm. We may have significant differences with some people in those outer rings. However, we can decide to look for the best in people and find common ground. No matter the barriers, we can choose to love one another; or as previously discussed, commit to each other's good.

This is hard work. We must intentionally choose to accept others as worthy. That does not mean we have to accept destructive behavior. We need to actively listen to one another. We may not agree but we can work hard to hear what lies in our hearts. As Stephen Covey said, we must seek first to understand, then to be understood. By choosing to lean into a deeper relationship with each other, we actually create space that allows love to open our eyes to what we have in common, instead of what divides us.

Wrapping Up

When I think of all the different types of relationships we can have in our lives, I am reminded of a precious moment many years ago. My youngest son Ryan was just a toddler. One afternoon, he was trying to work his way down the stairs with some guidance. He reached out for me and said in his quiet, little voice, "Hold me hand, case me fall." Those words have brought a smile to my face many times over the years.

That phrase also serves to remind me that we all need a hand at times. One of the hardest things for us to do as adults is to ask for help. Somewhere along the way, we become convinced that we are somehow weak or unworthy if we need someone else to help us. Almost everyone is willing to help someone else, yet we put up a wall around us when we could use some assistance ourselves. Brené Brown suggests that this mindset is a way we armor up against our self-worth issues. We mistakenly think that we increase our personal power if we never ask for help. In actuality, we are weakened by our distorted thinking. Neuropsychology continues to affirm that we are stronger as social beings working interdependently with each other.

Fundamentally, we can only live at our best when we are willing to embrace our need for each other. When we can see that asking for help allows others to ask as well, we give each other permission to tear down the walls that separate us and empower us to live together more fully. As I think back on that little hand grasping mine, I am deeply moved by the love and trust that represents. What we need now more than ever is a reminder to be there for each other as we take the next uncertain steps.

Activity

1. Do some of the IAT assessments: https://implicit.harvard.edu/implicit/takeatest.html

WORK

Another of life's most important components is work. From need theory, we know that everyone must have a sense of agency to create meaning in their lives. Jonathan Haidt speaks to this in the conclusion of his book, *The Happiness Hypothesis*, with these words:

> *Happiness is not something that you can find, acquire, or achieve directly. You have to get the conditions right and then wait. Some of those conditions are within you, such as coherence among the parts and levels of your personality. Other conditions require relationships to things beyond you: Just as plants need sun, water, and good soil to thrive, people need love, work, and a connection to something larger. It is worth striving to get the right relationships between yourselves and others, between yourselves and your work, and between yourself and something larger than yourself. If you get these relationships right, a sense of purpose and meaning will emerge.*[18]

Finding meaningful work is not necessarily about a job or career. We can do purposeful work outside of an occupation. The real power comes when we can align our sense of purpose with the work we do every day.

If we take a hard look at what drives us to use our talents and skills each day, we can get to the core of our purpose. Simon Sinek writes about knowing our Why as compared to our What and How. We often know what we are doing and sometimes

---

[18] Jonathan Haidt, *The Happiness Hypothesis: Ten Ways to Find Happiness and Meaning in Life* (London: Random House Business, 2021).

we know how we are doing it. Yet, unless we know our why, we are missing a crucial foundation for our lives. When I am working with educators, I often ask them two questions:

- Why do you teach?
- Why do you teach the way you teach?

If we exchange the word "teach" with the appropriate verb for anyone's work, these questions give us the opportunity to dive deeper into our purpose and reasons for what we do. Getting a clearer perspective on our intentions in our work can help us determine if our actions are congruent with our beliefs and values. When they are, we enable ourselves to perform within our integrity. If they are not, we create dysfunction, friction, and imbalance in our daily lives.

When we are incongruent with our actions and beliefs, it is important to determine what is not authentic with our true selves. What needs to be realigned? Are we acting in contrast to our values or are we relying on inaccurate or incomplete beliefs to guide our actions? If we continue to work in an unclear or disjointed manner, we minimize our ability to find meaning and fulfillment in our lives. Asking penetrating questions as to why we do things gives us space to assess our motives and adjust accordingly if necessary. This process can be difficult and painful at times, but the dividends are life changing. Here are some additional questions that can guide our work.

- What is our mission/purpose?
- What do we want to accomplish? What is the end goal?
- What is essential for the work?
- What does it need to look like/ sound like/ feel like while we seek to fulfill the mission?
- What core values will guide our process?
- How do we support each other through the work?

- How will we measure our success?
- What will we do if we are not successful?
- What will we do if we are?

Ultimately, we want to invest in pursuits that engage us fully and provide pathways for us to maximize our contributions to the world around us. As such, it is necessary for us to take the time to truly delve into the whys of our work.

Characteristics of Meaningful Work

Commitment vs Compliance

As a teacher, I have had a love/hate relationship with lesson plans. When I was required to do them, I was resentful and sometimes rebellious. I met the letter of the law (most of the time) and complied with what was asked of me. However, the further in my career I went, the more I realized that when I at least created a broad plan of what I wanted to accomplish that day or week, I felt more prepared and equipped to be effective in my teaching. My perspective shifted from a compliance mindset to a committed one.

Every day we are faced with a wide range of tasks and responsibilities that fit somewhere on the continuum of compliance to commitment. To be honest, most things we do fall somewhere in the middle of "have to" and "want to." In our work and relationships, we encounter daily situations that require us to assess our motivation to complete the job at hand. Sometimes it takes everything we have (and then some) to get through the task. Other times, we are surprised at how quickly the time went while we were doing the work.

From an individual point of view, we want to build our lives around people and opportunities that resonate with who we are and with what we believe. This takes intentional effort and substantial time to navigate our way through situations and decisions over our lifetime. When we have a choice to move toward a more committed foundation instead of a compliant one, we shift toward a more intrinsically enriching life.

From a leader's point of view, it is imperative that we create an environment where others can choose commitment over compliance. At a minimum, we can reduce the mandated elements of the work to only those things that are non-negotiable. As often as possible, we need to create an atmosphere of trust and autonomy so that others can wholeheartedly invest in their jobs.

No matter whether it's our personal or professional perspective, a life that is driven by commitment versus compliance is far more meaningful and fulfilling. Anything we can do to shift our lives toward the "want to" side of the continuum is worth the investment.

Taking this a little further, I am reminded of an episode of the Dare to Lead podcast where Brené Brown spoke with Pippa Grange, a British applied psychologist and author with substantial experience in sports psychology. In their conversation, they focused on the contrasts between regulation vs relationship, compliance vs connection, and fear vs faith.

Whether we are at school, work, or in any group setting, all these things are a part of the equation for effective and meaningful dynamics. However, if we build a culture entirely on regulation, our daily interactions will be stiff, sterile, and confining. If the focus is solely on compliance, the spirit of the organization will suffer, wither, and falter. If we let real fear remain unaddressed, people will lose hope, drive, and joy. To counterbalance this, we must partner each of these with the things that give the processes and procedures life and energy.

With regulation, we must keep in mind that the humans involved are far more important than the handbooks and documents that serve to guide an organization. When we lead through a people-centered approach, our way of doing business is inspired and infused by the relationships we nurture and sustain.

With compliance, we must create an environment of connection with the "spirit of the law" as well as "the letter of the law." When we focus on the heart of why we do what we do, we can embrace requirements with positive motivation instead of dread and resignation. As a friend of mine used to say, "If you want to, you don't have to." We must develop a "want to," or even better, a "get to" atmosphere.

With fear, we must acknowledge that our apprehensions and uncertainties are real. However, we must find the courage to meet our fears head-on with intentionality and hope. When we have faith in ourselves, others, and things bigger than ourselves, we open our eyes to possibilities and opportunities that are hidden by the shadows of our fears.

Essentially, if we focus on relationships, connection, and faith, we enliven the structures and frameworks that we create to manage life. It is necessary to have rules, guidelines, and laws to help guide or govern our interactions with one another, but we must never lose sight that the end goal is to live life abundantly and purposefully together. This is done best through a life of love and service. No one has ever said on their deathbed that they wish they had been more compliant.

Intrinsic Motivation

Another way to capture how to support meaningful work is to focus on the differences between intrinsic and extrinsic motivation. Daniel Pink explores these elements in his book *Drive*. He describes that the dominating principle in business for much of the past century has been to use extrinsic motivation techniques centered on reward and punishment.

History has shown that this can produce short-term measures of success but fails to be a sustainable system in the long run. Pink goes on to highlight research and evidence that began to emerge as early as the 1940s which show that intrinsic motivation has far more staying power over time. He elaborates on these three elements of intrinsic motivation[19]:

- Autonomy
- Mastery
- Purpose

Autonomy speaks to our need for independence and self-direction. Pink highlights that we seek to have autonomy in the tasks we choose to do, the use of our time, the techniques we can employ, and the team with which we can work.

Mastery focuses on our desire to continue to grow and refine our talents and skills. Having the freedom and pathways to hone our abilities empowers us and drives us to perform at higher levels.

Purpose is essentially the spiritual component of autonomy and mastery. It answers the why of our work. With the first two, we achieve independence. With purpose, we engage with interdependence. When we choose to use our skills and experiences in the service of others, we connect to something bigger than ourselves.

When we can embrace intrinsic motivation in our work environment, we create psychological space to invigorate productivity, empower creativity and innovation, and establish what is referred to as flow. We explore this in the next section.

---

[19] Daniel H. Pink, *Drive: The Surprising Truth about What Motivates US* (New York, NY: Riverhead Books, 2009).

Flow

Driving in town one day, it dawned on me how intricate the flow of traffic was. Hundreds of massive machines passed within just a few feet of each other in a constant stream of activity. On the whole, it was a sophisticated choreography of human interaction. Then, someone cut across two lanes to try and turn left from the far right. In this case, catastrophe was averted but not without major adrenaline rushes for all of those in that person's path (and generated a few choice words as well). Soon though, everyone reverted back to the steady pace of synchronized travel.

Statistically, being in a car is a safe option, particularly when you truly realize how often accidents don't happen. When drivers are attuned to the flow around them, pay attention to their environment, and are physically and mentally stable and engaged, it is quite amazing how well the system works. Strangely, when we are doing it right, it seems almost automatic and effortless.

Flow is a natural part of the world around us. Like a creek winding its way down a hill or the crashing of the ocean waves on the beach, we can find a definitive pattern at work. Our lives as humans are guided by similar currents and influences. If we pay attention to these flows, we can use these forces to direct and enhance our daily work.

Mihaly Csikszentmihalyi (pronounced me-high chick-sent-me-high), a Hungarian American psychologist brought the concept of flow to the world's attention. During his life, he wrote multiple books on his studies of the state of intense concentration, absorption, and enjoyment people can experience in work and play. He describes that the characteristics of flow include:[20]

- *Completely involved in what we are doing, focused, and concentrated.*
- *A sense of ecstasy-being outside everyday reality.*
- *Greater inner clarity- knowing what needs to be done, and how well we are doing.*
- *Knowing that the activity is doable – that our skills are adequate for the task.*
- *A sense of serenity – no worries about oneself, and a feeling of growing beyond the boundaries of the ego.*
- *Timelessness – thoroughly focused on the present, hours seem to pass by in minutes.*
- *Intrinsic motivation – whatever produces flow becomes its own reward.*

When we align our skill set with work that is appropriately challenging and worthwhile, we can create flow. In this state, we are able to bring joy and meaning to the daily tasks we perform. For instance, when I am in flow teaching a class or leading a workshop, I lose a sense of time and feel fully present with the others around me. I become aware of the energy in the room and feed off it. I intuitively find meaningful connections from the content to those I am teaching. When the lesson or presentation comes to an end, I feel a sense of closure and resolution.

Ignoring the synchronicity that plays out in our lives every day can be a dangerous thing. Just like the previously mentioned driver, when we ignore what is happening around us through ignorance, arrogance, or inattention, we put ourselves and others in harm's way. We can instead, through intentionality

---

[20] "Ted Talk – Mihaly Csikszentmihalyi – Flow – 2004," YouTube (YouTube, October 4, 2015), https://www.youtube.com/watch?v=I_u-Eh3h7Mo.

and practice, learn to "go with the flow" and live life more abundantly.

Teamwork

I heard this proverb quoted on a podcast: "If you want to go quickly, go alone; if you want to go far, go together."

Over my career, I have wrestled with the heart of these words. Like many others, I have often said that it is easier to just do it myself. I believe in some cases, not only is this true, but also necessary. However, those times are actually rarer than we think. Most of what we hope to accomplish in life requires us to work with others. Being a member of a team enables us to share the workload, maximize our individual strengths, and develop others to carry on the work when we move on to other endeavors.

One of the best things I did as a school leader was to build a team around me that could help carry the heaviness of the workload. While I struggled with thinking that others would see me as weak if I didn't do it all, I came to realize that it was impossible for me to live like that without destroying my quality of life. When I allowed others to take on significant parts of the necessary work at hand, it improved my personal health and, simultaneously, the health of the school.

Sharing the tasks and responsibilities with my team also gave each of us space to maximize our strengths. Being able to focus more specifically on fewer things enabled us to have more energy and time on work that was in our wheelhouse. Think of it like this. If my capacity tank is at 100% and I am spreading it over ten areas, each area is getting 10%. If I am on a team of five and each of us has 100% in our capacity tanks, then we can each take two areas and give 50% to them. Both those involved and the organization as a whole benefit.

Maybe the most important element of teams is the ability to develop others. When we are just trying to get the job done and out of the way, we miss the opportunity to expand the capacity of the people around us. When we take the time to train and mentor the next generation in our organizations, we are laying a substantial foundation for sustainability and growth.

Teamwork does take more time to develop fully. The concept of an infinite game may help to reframe the relationship between time and purpose. Simon Sinek speaks of James Carse's work on infinite games vs. finite games. A finite game has time limits, clearly defined endpoints, and fixed parameters. Infinite games never end, people move in and out of them, and success is measured not in wins and losses but in living fully and meaningfully. Football, chess, and tournaments are finite games; relationships, business, education, and life are infinite games.

Sometimes it is necessary to get a task finished quickly and efficiently. These situations play out regularly in finite games. However, in things that are timeless and priceless, relationship development pays greater dividends. We know deep down that we are meant to be social beings. We must intentionally take time, energy, and resources to build sustainable teams. A math mentor of mine once said, "We never have time to do it right, but we always seem to find time to do it twice." While it may seem that working purposefully with others takes too much time, for our work to have lasting and "infinite" consequences, we must invest in each other.

Leadership

What does it mean to lead? There are thousands of books on leadership. The definition looks different in almost every one of them. So, it is important for each of us to come to our own understanding of leadership. For me, two thoughts guide the way. First is this: Leadership is about influence, not control. Secondly, I heard a student at a scholarship interview give this answer to what leadership is: It's caring enough about something to take responsibility for it.

As a school leader over much of my career, I had to grow into my leadership style through trial and error. When I tried to use my "title" to get things done, it sometimes created immediate results but, almost always, with long-term, adverse effects. I came to value servant leadership as a more successful path to lead. When I began to look for ways to help others do their work more efficiently and remove unnecessary burdens put on them, I found that the whole school flourished and grew. Equipping and empowering others proved to be much more beneficial and meaningful.

Abby Wambach, a world-champion soccer player and author, has a powerful book on leadership called *Wolfpack*. She explores leadership principles in the context of her professional soccer career. One of the Wolfpack rules that spoke to me is "Leading from the Bench." Abby compares the old rule of waiting for permission to lead to the new rule of leading now – from wherever you are. She shares about the last few games of her career having to come off the bench. She had a choice. She could let the new circumstances dictate her life or she could step up and do what she could, given the new dynamics.

In my present life, I have stepped away from being the one in charge. While it has taken some time for me to process the change, it is even clearer to me now that real leadership is about influence. When we embrace this truth, we actually open the door to utilizing our skills and talents in meaningful ways. Even though we often have no direct control over the events going on around us, we can:

- Show up with an attitude of hope and gratitude
- Look for ways to serve
- Listen more intently
- Speak up when necessary
- Encourage others
- Extend grace to those with whom we disagree
- Find ways to strengthen and grow our relationships

We could create a huge list of options here. What is important is that we each choose to be present and involved daily. Use your influence to make a difference, big or small. If we all step up and do what we can, the cumulative impact will be phenomenal.

Wrapping Up

Essentially, we know that every human being needs to feel that they have something to offer the world. Our contributions come through work and service. When we determine what our "why" is in life, we empower our actions and words to provide beneficial and meaningful support for those around us. Friedrich Nietzsche said, "He who has a why to live can bear almost any how."

Our work only has meaning in the context of our relationships. When we engage interdependently, we create a synergy that drives connection and success. From this environment, teamwork and leadership reach new levels of impact. The real power in leadership comes from a servant mindset that focuses on influence instead of control.

Likewise, when we frame our work as part of an infinite system, we will come to realize that our time in any endeavor is temporary, However, our investment in the development and growth of others is eternal.

Activities

1. Take the PrinciplesYou assessment: https://principlesyou.com/
2. Take the 16 Personalities assessment: https://www.16personalities.com/

DAILY LIFE

The heart of the title of this book comes from a phrase attributed to Jesus. One version of the Bible words it this way "that they might have life, and that they might have it more abundantly."[21] As a young boy, this verse captured my attention. As we come to the final section of this book, I would like to focus on a few additional areas that can enhance our lives in "abundant" ways.

Well and Good

Be well and do good! This phrase has four essential words. Be vs. Do and Well vs. Good. My whole life I have wrestled with "I'm doing good" or "I'm doing well." Proper grammar differentiates that the first is an action to benefit something external. The second is a statement of our personal well-being. In either case, the challenges of life can lead us to take a hard look at these dynamics: doing and being. We all have heard or said some of these things: *I don't know what to do. There's nothing to do. What do I need to do? I should be doing something. I can't just sit around and do nothing.*

We have been conditioned to believe that we need to be doing something all the time. Our sense of self-worth for many of us is based on how much we get accomplished each day. Did we do enough? Did we do something worthwhile? Did we meet the daily quota for worthiness?

---

[21] John 10:10, King James Version

Similarly, we struggle with being. We rarely permit ourselves to just be. To be still, to be quiet, to be present, to be mindful, to be okay with not doing. If you are like me, I get restless easily. My mind is a hamster on a wheel a large part of the time, not able to stop long enough to just be. I feel guilty if I'm not actively doing something.

It doesn't have to be that way. Actually, for us to find balance physically, mentally, emotionally, and spiritually, we have to intentionally make time to stop and become aware of all that is pulsing through us. If that seems difficult, start with just a few minutes to breathe deeply and slowly. Integrate one or two things that can help you be mindful and reflective: walking, writing, singing, praying, meditating, exercising, climbing, talking, sharing, or whatever works for you. Listen to what your heart and mind are trying to say.

Doing is not a negative, though. However, if we are doing things out of the wrong context or for the wrong reasons, we will pay the costs eventually. It seems to me if we want our doing to be meaningful, we must come from a place of healthy being. We must purposely take time to calm the inner storm regularly. As we have discussed previously, some of us may need to seek help in doing that. All of us will need to be reminded consistently. When we find our way to just being for a short period of time, we can discern how to move forward with purpose and love.

Creating Meaningful Habits

For us to sustain an abundant life, we must have healthy habits in place that can support us through the best and worst of times. James Clear's book, *Atomic Habits*, emphasizes the science and art of creating the daily routines that help us stay aligned with our true selves. He says that we do not rise to the level of our goals, we fall to the level of our systems. Our systems are the habits that are ingrained into our lives on a daily basis. Clear highlights that there is a habit loop that underlies our actions. We are influenced by these four phases:[22]

1. Cue
2. Craving
3. Response
4. Reward

For instance, at the grocery store we might see a Take Five candy bar at the checkout register. That's the cue. The craving is that sudden laser-like focus on how good that would taste. Our response could be to pick up one or two and toss them into our basket. The reward is that first bite out in the car on the way home.

This neurological feedback loop can be manipulated intentionally. Clear delineates four elements that help us create good habits:

- Make it obvious
- Make it attractive
- Make it easy
- Make it satisfying

This is exemplified by how the stores place impulse buys at the checkout lanes. If we are trying to break bad habits, Clear reframes the prior steps through their opposites:

- Make it invisible
- Make it unattractive
- Make it difficult
- Make it unsatisfying

---

[22] James Clear, *Atomic Habits* (Penguin USA, 2019).

An example of this for me was when I stopped drinking soft drinks. We placed the sodas in the bottom of our pantry, out of sight, and only kept a few for visitors. I started avoiding the drink aisle in the store. I focused on the fact that my blood work revealed prediabetes. This made the thought of drinking a Coke very unattractive.

Establishing a healthy system of habits is critical to living a full and fulfilling life. If that is missing in our lives, getting there is not as overwhelming as it appears. It is important to realize that we can make substantial changes in our lives by adjusting a little every day.

Let's look at two mathematical models. Clear talks about making 1% changes. If we could just do one small action every day to improve our lives, the end result can be astonishing. Here is the pattern:

We start with all that we are on a given day, represented by 1 or 100%. A one percent change can be modeled by multiplying by 100% + 1% or 1.01. So, the pattern would look like this:

First day 1 x 1.01= 1.01. We carry the 1.01 to the next day.

2nd day 1.01 x 1.01 = 1.0201 And carry the 1.0201 to the next day.

3rd day 1.0201 x 1.01 = 1.0303

And so on. Early on, the changes are small – the difference between 1.00 and 1.03 is so small that it may be barely noticeable. However, if we keep this up every day for a year we get

$$1 \times (1.01)^{365} = 37.78$$

That's almost 38 times more than what we started with. While the math may be distracting, this speaks to how integrating a little every day can have an astronomical impact over time.

Another model that illustrates this comes from Martha Beck. She speaks of one-degree turns to help move us toward aligning with our integrity. Throughout this book, we have talked about being congruent with our true selves. Depending on the context of our lives, we may be fully aligned or, possibly, way off-center. If we need to move toward balance, making one-degree turns every day will eventually bring us to congruence. Beck uses a plane in flight to highlight the power of small changes. If a pilot needs to alter a flight plan, they can make small one-degree moves to alter the course, instead of a hard turn. Over time, the course corrections will align with the new destination. If we choose to make little changes toward the life we want to live, we will find ourselves closer to wholeness and balance.

Permission to Struggle

I don't want to minimize that the work of aligning with our true selves is difficult at times and is essentially a never-ending process. But so is breathing. We will stumble and fall regularly, but if we keep striving for congruence, we will reap life-changing benefits. When we are faced with overwhelming circumstances, we can do some things to help:

- Give ourselves permission to stumble our way through it. There will be times and circumstances in our lives where no one has a predetermined answer. Trial and error might be the only way to work through them. Our main responsibility is to learn from our experiences as quickly as possible.
- Be realistic in our expectations for those involved, particularly ourselves. Trying to be perfect or expecting others to be is unhealthy and unnecessary.

- Put people first. We need to be aware of the emotional strain uncertainty creates and be gracious to each other in the process.
- Determine what is essential and prioritize those things.
- When all is said and done each day, we need to realize we've done the best we can in the circumstances. Tomorrow, we can give it another go.

If we are willing to listen to the wisdom of others, do the hard work of learning who we are and what makes us tick, and put into practice the effective and purposeful steps toward physical, mental, emotional, and spiritual health, we can navigate through the daily storms and uncertainties that we all face. No matter what we encounter, those situations are temporary, and they do not define us. Pema Chödrön puts it poetically: We are not the weather, we are the sky.[23]

On another Dare to Lead podcast, Brené Brown asked Susan David, "What is one piece of leadership advice that is so remarkable that you need to share it?" David said, "Help people to trust the compass, not the map."[24] This really struck me deeply. I have relied wholeheartedly on maps in my life as a traveler. In addition, I have created "maps" of my experiences in life that have guided my decision-making process. In many cases, I have chosen certain paths in my life based primarily on "the way I have always done it." However,

---

[23] Eric Barker, "This Is How to Have Emotionally Intelligent Relationships: 4 Secrets from Research," Barking Up The Wrong Tree, March 22, 2022, https://www.bakadesuyo.com/2022/01/emotionally-intelligent-relationships/.

[24] "Brené with Dr. Susan David on the Dangers of Toxic Positivity, Part 1 of 2," Brené Brown, March 14, 2023, https://brenebrown.com/podcast/brene-with-dr-susan-david-on-the-dangers-of-toxic-positivity-part-1-of-2/.

if dealing with the global Covid pandemic has taught us anything, it's that life can change in a heartbeat.

Many of the previous "maps" that we have used to navigate life can become suddenly useless, irrelevant, or outdated. To address the seismic shift in our lives, we must adjust quickly, coming up with new procedures and routines. We must rely on our values and beliefs to construct pathways through the chaos and confusion. While we may go through substantial pain and grief in the process, we can discover new skills and strengths we may not have known we possessed.

The lessons from the pandemic apply to every day of our lives. No matter what has occurred up to this point in our life journey, we can choose to make changes on any given day. Letting go of outdated maps and using one percent or one-degree decisions can help us adjust our life trajectory toward wholeness and balance.

CONCLUSION

When I look back at my life so far, I have so much to be thankful for. My journey to become my true self has not been linear. However, every path I have taken, both good and bad, has helped make me the man I am today. While I certainly don't believe there is such a thing as a perfect life, I do believe in perfect moments. Those are the times in our lives that we can say that it doesn't get any better than this. Looking back over the years, the majority of those moments revolved around me being my authentic self while being invested in loving relationships. If we can string together more of those types of experiences into our daily lives, we can build an abundant life.

To do this, we have to be intentional about it. I like to think of maintaining congruence with our true selves as tuning an instrument. I have found that if I adjust my guitar regularly each week, I only need to make small changes to stay in tune. However, when I let it sit for months, it often takes a substantial amount of twisting and tweaking to find that sought-after pitch. Sometimes, it requires a whole new stringing to get back to where I want it to be.

So, it is with finding ourselves, accepting ourselves, and giving ourselves away. If we can spend a little time every day assessing whether we are balanced across the physical, mental, emotional, and spiritual strands of our lives and doing the minor adjustments necessary, we will be empowered to live each day abundantly and to give of ourselves fully to the world in loving and compassionate ways. When we take the small steps daily, we will find that, over time, we will have made major strides toward a meaningful and purposeful life.

RECOMMENDED READING

Richard Bach *Jonathan Livingston Seagull*

Martha Beck *The Way of Integrity*

Brené Brown

      Dare to Lead

      The Gifts of Imperfection

      Atlas of the Heart

      Daring Greatly

      Braving the Wilderness

      Rising Strong

Gary Chapman *The 5 Love Languages*

Paulo Coelho *The Alchemist*

Stephen Covey *The Seven Habits of Highly Effective People*

John and Julia Gottman *The Love Prescription*

Adam Grant *Think Again*

Jonathan Haidt *The Happiness Hypothesis*

bell hooks *all about love*

Ibram X Kendi *How to be an Antiracist*

Trina Paulus *Hope for the Flowers*

Daniel Pink

    Drive

    Regrets

Scott Peck *The Road Less Traveled*

Simon Sinek *Infinite Game*

BIBLIOGRAPHY

Clear, James. *Atomic Habits*. Penguin USA, 2019.

Writers, UCHealth. "Five Reasons Water Is so Important to Your Health." UCHealth Today, November 2, 2021. https://www.uchealth.org/today/five-reasons-water-is-so-important-to-your-health/.

Barker, Eric. "This Is How to Have Emotionally Intelligent Relationships: 4 Secrets from Research." Barking Up The Wrong Tree, March 22, 2022. https://www.bakadesuyo.com/2022/01/emotionally-intelligent-relationships/.

"Brené with Dr. Susan David on the Dangers of Toxic Positivity, Part 1 of 2." Brené Brown, March 14, 2023. https://brenebrown.com/podcast/brene-with-dr-susan-david-on-the-dangers-of-toxic-positivity-part-1-of-2/.

Koop, Fermin. "Not Too Hot, Not Too Cold. What's the Ideal Room Temperature?" ZME Science, March 9, 2023. https://www.zmescience.com/other/feature-post/not-too-hot-not-too-cold-whats-the-ideal-room-temperature/.

"American Heart Association Recommendations for Physical Activity in Adults and Kids." www.heart.org, July 28, 2022. https://www.heart.org/en/healthy-living/fitness/fitness-basics/aha-recs-for-physical-activity-in-adults?gclid=Cj0KCQjw-

ABOUT THE AUTHOR

With over thirty-eight years of experience as an educator, coach, and leader in diverse roles and settings, Tim seeks to use his journey to encourage and support others in reaching their goals and living out their purpose. He has served as a teacher, counselor, principal, director, state consultant, and life and leadership coach over his career. His work has been across elementary, middle, and high school as well as adjunct teaching at the collegiate level. He has a BA in Mathematics, an MA in School Counseling, and EdD in Educational Leadership, all from Western Kentucky University. He is an ACC-certified life coach with the International Coach Federation. When not teaching or coaching, he enjoys hiking, fishing, kayaking, disc golf, carpentry, and juggling. He and his wife, Ellen, live in Smyrna, Tennessee, and have three great kids who are married and living life abundantly.

Printed in the USA
CPSIA information can be obtained
at www.ICGtesting.com
LVHW071524090823
754638LV00017B/388